MW00532235

Praise for *The Purposeful Wealth Advisor*

"With equal parts logic and love, Raj Sharma makes a convincing case that working as a financial advisor is a noble and lucrative career. He offers a clear step-by-step guide to becoming an advisor, thriving in the role, and helping clients live richer, more fulfilling lives."

—**Jack Otter,**
editor-at-large, *Barron's*;
global head, Dow Jones Wealth & Asset Management

"As one of Merrill Lynch's most successful financial advisors, Raj is now sharing his wisdom and experience. This book is a must-read for someone considering a career in wealth management."

—**Winthrop H. Smith Jr.,**
retired chairman, Merrill Lynch International

"Financial independence and management are core to a woman's success, and Raj Sharma shows us just how to accomplish this by sharing a wealth of information and strategies to be successful. Raj's commitment to giving back to society is exemplified in his approach to wealth management—thoughtful, strategic, and results-oriented. I hope this book inspires more women and minorities to consider the advisory profession."

—**Lata Krishnan,**
technology entrepreneur and philanthropist

"A good read for all investment professionals that shows how to overcome challenges. We extend our well-done to Raj Sharma for underscoring his focus on the client. A clear, undeterred, and steadfast focus on how to serve client needs and communicate, communicate, and communicate."

—**Mario Gabelli,**
founder, chairman, and CEO, Gabelli Asset Management

"I have known Raj Sharma for nearly thirty years, and during that time I've come to know him as one of the most thoughtful and most sincere financial advisors in the business. *The Purposeful Wealth Advisor* fully reflects those admirable attributes and highlights that a financial advisor's personal success is largely achieved by focusing on their clients' and society's well-being."

—Richard Bernstein,
CEO and chief investment officer,
Richard Bernstein Advisors

"A critical skill for individual success is developing strategies for wealth accumulation and management. That is greatly facilitated with a trusted financial advisor. Raj's journey to wealth management success provides key insights, not only to aspiring wealth managers, but also to clients seeking an advisor with whom they can jointly succeed. From humble beginnings and many challenges, Raj provides fresh perspectives on the importance of a purposeful advisor."

—Eric Rosengren,
former president, Federal Reserve Bank of Boston

"This book is a *must-read* for anyone who wants to succeed, not just in the financial services wealth management sector, but across all industries and disciplines. Raj Sharma has written the quintessential handbook on how to succeed, whether in corporate America, as an entrepreneur, or in life—particularly if you are a person of color, an immigrant, or a woman. How does a young immigrant from India end up being one of America's top wealth advisors? In his book, Raj Sharma shows us how to be successful by following a few simple principles: *a spirit of optimism, a sense of gratitude and humility, respect for yourself and others,* and *honesty and transparency*. This book is a living testament to the immigrant story and how immigrants are contributing to America's economic ecosystem while at the same time showing their gratitude through philanthropy—proving that America really is the land of opportunity."

—Colette A. M. Phillips,
president and CEO, Colette Phillips Communications;
founder, Get Konnected!; co-founder, the GK Fund

"This book is an invaluable resource for all wealth advisors, would-be wealth advisors, and business executives. In this inspiring immigrant success story, Raj Sharma shows us exactly what has enabled him to go from his humble beginnings to being one of the most successful wealth advisors in America. Raj has written a necessary and timely book, delivering a road map for unlimited success."

—Ajay Banga,
vice chairman, General Atlantic;
former CEO and executive chairman, Mastercard

"In *The Purposeful Wealth Advisor*, Raj sends a powerful message about the urgency for more nontraditional entrants into the advisory field to provide the kind of guidance and advice that can leave a positive and lasting impact on people's financial futures."

—Saira Malik,
chief investment officer, Nuveen

THE PURPOSEFUL WEALTH ADVISOR

www.amplifypublishing.com

The Purposeful Wealth Advisor: How to Build a Rewarding Career While Helping Clients Achieve Their Dreams

For more information on Top Advisor Recognition List disclosures, please visit https://mediahandler.broadridgeadvisor.com/media/366567/MerrillBroadridgeAwardDisclosure.pdf.

Second printing. This Amplify Publishing edition printed in 2022.

For more information, please contact:
Amplify Publishing, an imprint of Amplify Publishing Group
620 Herndon Parkway #320
Herndon, VA 20170
info@amplifypublishing.com

Library of Congress Control Number: 2022907349

CPSIA Code: PRV0822B
ISBN-13: 978-1-63755-548-4

Printed in the United States

To Nalini, my life partner and best friend, soul mate, collaborator—and, of course, insightful critic.

THE PURPOSEFUL WEALTH ADVISOR

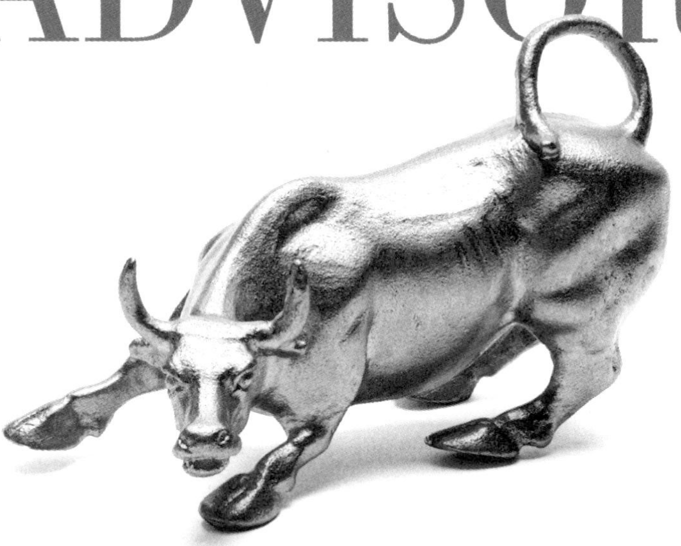

HOW TO BUILD A REWARDING CAREER WHILE HELPING CLIENTS ACHIEVE THEIR DREAMS

RAJ SHARMA

Named to *Barron's* Hall of Fame
Ranked by *Barron's* and *Forbes* as a Top 100 Wealth Advisor

Foreword by Andy Sieg,
president, Merrill Wealth Management

CONTENTS

FOREWORD

The wealth management business today is evolving as the industry responds to growing investor needs. At Merrill, we see the current bull market for advice continuing as Americans seek professional guidance to help them achieve their goals while managing the uncertainties in the world around them. This bullish outlook for our profession makes *The Purposeful Wealth Advisor* a timely and valuable guide to a successful career as a financial advisor.

Raj Sharma is uniquely qualified to author such a book. Joining Merrill Lynch in August 1987, two months before the Black Monday crash, he set out undeterred and determined to learn everything about wealth management. In the ensuing thirty-five years, Raj has set a consistent standard of excellence, built a phenomenally successful advisory business, helped countless clients achieve their goals and dreams, and attained legendary status across our industry.

This excellence has continually earned Raj recognition both externally and internally, and he pays it forward—mentoring dozens of young advisors over the course of his career and by giving generously to his community and to a myriad of global causes.

Raj personifies the best of Merrill's culture, and in *The Purposeful Wealth Advisor* he leads readers step by step along his path, from learning why and how to create an advisor brand, to setting goals, to building a top-notch team focused on doing more and being better for clients.

Whether you are an experienced advisor, just starting, or are considering a career in financial services, *The Purposeful Wealth Advisor* has something to offer. Raj Sharma has crowned his outstanding career with a gift that serves to inspire the current and next generation of financial advisors to excel as they enable millions of people to reach their hopes and dreams.

Andy Sieg,
president, Merrill Wealth Management
March 2022

INTRODUCTION

Becoming a financial advisor changed my life. I stumbled into this profession by accident, but it has inspired and sustained me for over three decades now. It's not an exaggeration to say that my work has given meaning and purpose to my life.

I am incredibly grateful to Merrill Lynch for giving me an opportunity to develop a career, build a business, and create the life of my dreams. Every step of the way, the firm has been supportive of my practice, thanks to the wonderful "Mother Merrill" philosophy that still pervades the organization. Merrill Lynch has a culture of celebrating success and caring for each other by freely sharing ideas and best practices. I'm grateful that when Bank of America acquired Merrill Lynch they saw the value in our name and our culture and retained it. Together we've become a financial service powerhouse unmatched in our scope and impact around the world.

In many ways, this firm represents the best of our country. America is a land of aspiration and dreams, irrespective of who you are or where you were born. This has defined our national ethos, and I hope this essential characteristic never changes. We are not perfect. But more so than any other country, we are capable of self-reflection and change.

I often tell young people that no career is linear or predictable. My career took me in several directions. I got my bachelor's degree in business and economics in Hyderabad, India, and started out in sales. After a while, I got my MBA and spent two years at a major industrial firm, gaining valuable experience in marketing and finance.

Throughout my time in business in India, I also worked part time as an English-language radio DJ. That experience led me to head west and get a master's degree in mass communication at Emerson College in Boston. I worked in film and video production for a couple of years, attempted to start a gourmet coffee company—long before Starbucks came on the scene—and eventually stumbled into financial advisory when my own stockbroker suggested I'd be well suited to the field.

Throughout my life and career, there are a few principles I have lived by:

- A spirit of optimism: I am one of the most optimistic people in the world. I have always believed cynicism and skepticism are obstacles to progress and achievement. Optimism does not mean I am unrealistic or Pollyannaish or that I overlook challenges. Optimism is a way of looking at life through the prism of positive expectation. This unerring sense of optimism sustains me as a person. I also feel that it generates positive energy and motivates people around me.

- A sense of gratitude and humility: No one achieves success on their own. We all need someone to pack our parachute. I try to express my gratitude every single day for everything that life has given me. Among other things, I am grateful to be a citizen of this wonderful country that has done so much good in the world.

- A sense of respect: Treating every single person with respect is something that my parents taught me. I do not believe any person is superior as a human being because of their position in life.

- Leading with honesty and transparency: There is nothing more powerful than being honest, transparent, and direct, whether it is in the business world or in your personal life.

Nothing worthwhile is ever achieved without hard work and persistence. It has taken me over three decades to become an overnight success. Throughout my career, my wife, Nalini, has been a steadfast business and life partner, constantly encouraging me to do my best. I am so grateful for our love and friendship. In 2022, we celebrated our forty-second wedding anniversary. We are also blessed with four wonderful children: Meara, Neil, Jay, and Tara.

This book is my expression of gratitude to a business and company that has given me so much. I hope my story will inspire more young people to consider wealth management as a career—in particular women and minorities, who are woefully underrepresented in the entire financial services industry. I strongly believe wealth management is an exciting, fulfilling, and entrepreneurial career for anyone who has the drive and persistence to succeed.

Over the past thirty years, I have seen hundreds of advisors fail and leave the business. Every day I witness advisors who are struggling to grow and succeed. And I see numerous others, despite being successful, who have not truly articulated their purpose. By sharing my insights, mistakes, and best practices, I hope to help more advisors approach their practice with purpose and intentionality, enabling them to thrive and succeed.

I intend to donate the net proceeds of this book to nonprofit financial planning organizations that are dedicated to serving low-income families, empowering them with the knowledge and tools to become financially literate and independent. I firmly believe our society and country will be stronger with responsible wealth management and wider access to such programs.

1

MYTHS AND MISPERCEPTIONS ABOUT THE ADVISORY BUSINESS

Dare to live the life you have dreamed for yourself. Go forward and make your dreams come true.

—Ralph Waldo Emerson

If I ask you to think about a financial advisor, what kind of person comes to mind? What does that person look like? Where did they go to school? How do they find their clients? What are they good at?

If you're like most people, you probably pictured a white man in his fifties, a man who went to an Ivy League school and has a lot of rich friends and relatives who send clients his way. Maybe you imagined this guy was a math whiz who spends most of his time poring over spreadsheets and calculating compound interest.

If that's the picture that comes to mind when I say the words *financial advisor*, in some ways you're right about the state of the industry today—mostly older, white, and male. More on that later. But for now I want to tell you all the ways you're wrong about who a financial advisor *should* be. Throughout this book, I will use the terms *financial advisor*, *advisor*, and *wealth management advisor* to describe my role in the industry. All these terms describe someone whose primary role is to provide holistic financial advice to clients, including but not limited to investment advice.

There are a lot of myths and misperceptions about the wealth management business. Hollywood helps perpetuate these myths. In the movies, it's somehow still the greed-is-good 1980s, and financial advisors are all men in suits yelling into phones. Maybe today they're talking about collateralized debt obligations, but the men, the suits, the yelling—the basic idea—hasn't changed.

In reality, the industry has changed a lot since the 1980s, when I got my start. But too many people are still holding on to outdated ideas of what it takes to succeed as an advisor.

Let's walk through some of the most common myths and misperceptions about the business.

Myth: you must have connections with wealthy people in order to succeed in the advisory business.

Truth: Having connections might open a few doors for you, but it's not a guarantee of success. Finding an advisor is like finding a good primary care doctor—people are looking for competence, care, and integrity. Anyone with those qualities can build a strong business as an investment advisor.

And you definitely don't have to have a rich uncle to find clients. For one thing, it's not only people who are already rich who need help managing their investments. About 55 percent of all Americans own some stock.[1] That number is down a little bit since the financial crisis but has held relatively steady since then. Especially if you're just starting in the business, you don't have to concentrate exclusively on connecting with wealthy people. Your clients can grow with you.

I certainly was far from rubbing elbows with the rich and famous when I started in the business. As a student at Emerson, I briefly had a negative net worth. Leaving class one day, my car wouldn't move, because it had a big yellow boot on it! I owed $1,300 in outstanding tickets, and I only had $300 in the bank. I had to take a loan from a friend to pay off my tickets and release my car.

My situation was a little better when I actually started working at Merrill, but I was still far from wealthy. We needed a second car around that time, so I bought a used Volkswagen Rabbit for $600. For that price, the car was a bargain. It ran perfectly well. There was just one problem: the driver-side door didn't open, so I had to crawl in through the passenger side. I used that car to drive to presentations with prospective clients. One day I took it to a seminar on retirement planning for a group of doctors. The presentation went well, and I'd actually closed the sale, but the head of the group wanted to walk me to my car. I had to pretend I had to take a call from the office so he wouldn't see me crawling into my $600 car!

If you're in a similar phase of your life, rest assured there are plenty of ways to make connections with potential clients that don't involve spending an afternoon on a golf course at a fancy country

1 Lydia Saad and Jeffrey M. Jones, "What Percentage of Americans Owns Stock?," Gallup, August 13, 2021, https://news.gallup.com/poll/266807/percentage-americans-owns-stock.aspx.

club. I'll share some strategies that have worked for me in another section, but for now just know I've never played a single round of golf to meet a prospective client. It's not efficient! Besides, I am a terrible golfer.

Myth: You must be aggressive to do well in this business.

Truth: This is a classic stereotype perpetuated in Hollywood movies, like *Wall Street* and *The Wolf of Wall Street*. Today's reality is totally different. To be an effective advisor, you need to focus on thoughtful planning and strategy, not aggressive sales tactics.

The business has changed a lot over the years, and strategies that might have brought short-term success in the past just won't work today. When I first started out, in the late 1980s, I was told that cold-calling was the only way to build a practice. Back then, advisors were stockbrokers. They were paid on commission every time their clients placed a trade, whether it was a purchase or sale of a stock or bond. They were not paid to monitor and maintain a portfolio. The incentives were certainly misaligned.

In those days, stockbrokers were trained to be as aggressive as possible. A typical cold-calling script would go something like this: "I'm calling you about *X* stock. It's at five dollars a share now, and we think it's going to fifty dollars. *Are you man enough* to buy five thousand shares?" This was a line from a company that went bankrupt during the great financial crisis of 2008.

I hated that culture. I rejected the idea of cold-calling and pressuring people to buy specific stocks from day one. I remember, early in my career, talking to a manager about my search for a house. I'd saved up, and I'd decided that with my budget I could afford a $300,000 house. But this manager told me that I should take out a $500,000 mortgage because I'd be under so much pressure to make the payments that I'd be sure to succeed.

That was the mindset back then—push yourself, push your clients, take risks. But it wasn't my mindset. I ended up buying a house for $274,000. I didn't want to be under that constant pressure to keep my numbers up. I wanted to build a sustainable business that matched my values.

Some people thought I was crazy. Some people loved that sales-based, commission-based business environment. Some people did really well for themselves under that model. I remember I tried to get some advice from a senior stockbroker on my second day at work, and he barked at me, "Don't bother me when I'm working! Call me after four!"

That guy was very successful under the old commission-based model—and clearly he knew it. But he wouldn't succeed today. In fact, he got out of the business when it switched to a fee-based model that rewarded people with a less aggressive, more consultative style.

Merrill Lynch, where I've made my career, was one of the first firms to offer a fee structure, in which clients were charged based on their total assets under management rather than paying commission on every trade. In many ways, Merrill was a pioneer and a trendsetter in the business.

I eagerly embraced this change. But I remember one successful broker—a big, garrulous guy who worked for a major competitor—telling me, "Kid, what you're doing with this asset-based thing—why would you do that? You're making a big mistake."

And it was true. My income fell by about 50 percent in the first year after I switched. Think of it this way: If a client had $100,000 in their account, you could easily make $4,000 in commissions on that account in a year. But in an asset-based model, you'd only charge them $1,000. But I knew I couldn't sleep at night if my business wasn't based around doing what was best for my clients, but rather what was best for my bottom line. So I made the switch.

That big-time broker who told me that I was making a mistake remained successful for many years. But even as the industry changed around him, he stuck to his aggressive, high-risk strategies. You could come to him with $5 million, and he'd put your money in five individual stocks. He might make great money for you when things were good, but in the dot-com crash of 2000, his portfolios lost about 70 percent. Clients walked out on him. Some sued him for building insufficiently diversified portfolios. He ultimately left the business.

That kind of aggressive approach might have worked in the past. It might even win you short-term success today. But it's simply no longer true that you have to be aggressive to build a sustainable career as a wealth manager. In fact, the opposite is true. Today you have to be a good listener, a faithful custodian of your clients' best interests, and a calm port in a storm when stocks start to slide, and clients get nervous.

Myth: managing money is the province of men, and most financial decisions in a family are made by men.

Truth: Again, this might have been true for an older generation. But today men and women are equal decision-makers when it comes to financial matters. Indeed, according to *U.S. News* and *Money*, a recent survey found that 51 percent of women consider themselves the "CFO" of their household. More women today come into a relationship with their own resources. Many manage their investments separately from their spouse or partner.

Understanding and working with both partners is crucial whenever you have married or partnered clients. I have two clients, both physicians, who were married for many years and decided to split up after they retired. They called me to talk through their situation and ask what their financial lives would look like if they split their assets fifty-fifty. I was very careful to remain neutral in this conversation and to focus on the facts. I reminded them that they were both my friends, and my only role was to be a sounding board and to help them work through the financial consequences of any decision. Of course, they used mediators and lawyers to firm up their mutual agreement.

They're now divorced—and they're both still clients. Their children are my clients. In fact, the ex-wife has referred her new boyfriend to me, and he's now a client too!

Ignoring one partner in a relationship just because she's a woman, or because he or she makes less money, isn't just morally wrong—it's bad business. If you focus only on one partner's ideas and needs, you will lose that account. You may lose both partners quickly because they don't appreciate your attitude, or you may lose the wife you ignored after the husband dies. No matter what, you will lose business.

Myth: You must be a math whiz or an MBA to work in wealth management.

Truth: This one might be true—if you plan to be a quantitative analyst. But if you want to be a financial planner or wealth advisor, your ability to communicate, build trust, and develop a rapport with clients is far more important than your number-crunching skills. In many ways, EQ trumps IQ in this field.

I do have an MBA, but I've come to believe psychology majors make the best advisors. I've seen them have phenomenal success in this field. Advisors will always have to understand how markets work, dig into the pros and cons of different products, and so on. But being a great advisor is all about understanding clients' hopes, dreams, and fears. It's about asking good questions and pushing people to think more deeply about their life goals. It's about supporting your clients when the markets slide, and they worry they won't meet their goals. Of course, you want to build a strong business, and we'll discuss that more in succeeding chapters, but the foundation of your business is always going to be your relationships with your clients. Nothing matters more.

Myth: Wall Street only hires from Ivy League schools.

Truth: This might be true if you aspire to work in investment banking or capital markets. But most of the top advisors today probably went to state colleges or lesser-known schools. Your persistence, desire to succeed, hard work, and ability to communicate are far more important than having a big name on your résumé.

When it comes to education, what matters more than where you went for undergrad is your commitment to ongoing education. I believe becoming a Certified Financial Planner, getting a CIMA certification from the Institute of Management Consultants, or getting other certifications can be invaluable. These certifications can signify trust to your potential clients. They also help you constantly upgrade your knowledge and proficiency in the business.

The Myth of the Robo-Advisor

As of 2020, robots were managing about $460 billion—an increase of 30 percent from 2019. The appeal is simple: Robo-advisors—tech companies that use algorithms to manage investments—are cheap. They typically have very low minimum investment thresholds, and they charge low fees, so they are an attractive option for young people who haven't yet accumulated much in the way of assets. Of course, wealthier investors may also appreciate these companies' low fees and clear, rule-based investment systems.

If you're essentially a passive investor, a robo-advisor can do the basics of what you'd pay a human financial advisor much more to do. These algorithms can set up a basic balanced portfolio that's in line with the dominant portfolio construction theories most advisors use. They can periodically rebalance that portfolio to maintain the desired risk level and account for gains or losses in certain asset classes. They can even execute some basic tax prep strategies, such as tax-loss harvesting. And they sometimes come with other tools, like online retirement calculators, that will give you a rough idea of your progress toward your goals.

But let's talk about what robo-advisors *can't* do. Algorithms can't look at your financial life holistically. The services I provide my clients go way beyond creating a balanced portfolio and doing a little tax-loss harvesting. I talk to my clients about their entire financial lives. I help them with estate planning, I talk about the pros and cons of buying a second home, I help them think through prenups for their kids. Granted, not all financial advisors provide all these services, but we all do more than just create a portfolio.

Robots can't develop an intuitive feeling about your risk profile. Any advisor, human or robot, will walk clients through a series of questions to determine their risk tolerance and design a portfolio from there. But people are complicated. I often have clients who initially tell me that they're willing to accept more risk for more upside potential. But when I dig deeper, I learn they actually don't want to accept more than a 5 percent loss in any given year. That's not a lot of risk. An online quiz can put a number to your risk tolerance, but only a human can talk to you and start to understand your true feelings about fluctuations in the market.

Robots can't talk you through a crisis. When the market inevitably slumps, my team and I are on the phones around the clock, talking to our clients. Clients want to know what a correction means for their portfolios, and not just in numerical terms. They want to know: Will I still meet my goals? Is this normal? How long will this last? Should I be doing something? They need a calm voice on the other end of the phone or video call, reminding them that corrections are normal and encouraging them to stick to the plan.

An algorithm can't push you to think deeper. Robo-advisors can help you plan and save for certain basic goals, like retirement or a child's education. But with my clients, I don't just talk about goals. I talk about *purpose*. I ask every client: What's the purpose of your wealth? I encourage them to think about philanthropy and giving back if that's not already a priority. I'll talk about this aspect of my work with clients in greater detail in the ensuing chapters. But even advisors who don't ask these specific questions can encourage clients to think about things that might not otherwise have occurred to them. A computer can only work with the information you give it. A human can challenge you and keep an eye on your blind spots.

There are many myths and misperceptions about the advisory business, including the perception that, in a world of artificial intelligence, we no longer need human advisors. But I believe there is more opportunity today than ever before in this business. It's one of the most rewarding careers in the world. You don't need to invest a cent of your personal capital—all you need is grit, hard work, and a desire to make a difference in the lives of your clients. As far as I'm concerned, the field is wide open, and there has never been a better time to be a financial advisor.

Key Takeaways

- The financial advising industry is currently male-dominated and mostly white, and this is overdue for change.
- That creates an opportunity for women and people of color.
- It's a myth that you must know rich people in order to succeed in the business.
- It's a myth that you must be an aggressive salesperson in order to succeed. Today you need to be an advisor—a resource.
- It's also a myth that you must come from an Ivy League background.
- You don't have to be a math whiz either. Understanding human emotion and psychology is more important.
- A robo-advisor won't replace you anytime soon, because there are many things a robo-advisor can't do, such as reassure clients in the middle of a market correction.

2

A WORLD OF OPPORTUNITY

The statistics are shocking: Only 3.8 percent of certified financial planners are Black or Latinx, and fewer than 20 percent of advisors are women.[2] Within the financial advisory industry as a whole, more than 80 percent of advisors are white, and more than 80 percent are male. At Merrill Lynch, as of 2020, 4.5 percent of advisors were Black, 9 percent were Latinx, 23 percent were people of color, and 21 percent were female. I'm proud to say the firm continues to make diversity an important focus.

These numbers actually represent improvement from an even

2 Andrew Osterland, "Financial advisor industry, overwhelmingly White and male, seeks to overcome lack of diversity," CNBC, October 8, 2020, https://www.cnbc.com/2020/10/06/financial-advisory-industry-seeks-to-overcome-lack-of-racial-diversity.html#:~:text=CNBC%3A%20How%20diverse%20is%20the%20financial%20advisory%20industry%3F&text=Industry%2Dwide%2C%2082%25%20of,CFPs%20were%20Black%20or%20Latino.

more overwhelmingly white and male past, but clearly there's a lot more work to be done. An industry can't diversify overnight. Those of us in the wealth management profession need to be thinking about how to reach out to more young women and people of color to get them interested in the profession. We need to be focused on diversity not only in hiring, at all levels, but in mentoring. Women and minorities entering this profession will be forging their own paths, and we need to support them.

Diversifying Wealth Management and Diversifying Wealth Go Hand in Hand

It's no accident that the wealth management industry is dominated by white men. So is wealth. The income gap between Black and white families has been stuck at about $25,000 to $30,000—adjusted for inflation—for forty years.[3] In terms of assets, the median white family has about $123,000 in wealth, while the median Black family has only $23,000, or about 12 cents on the dollar, compared to white families.[4]

For women, the gender pay gap has been almost as persistent. Women still earn 82 cents on the dollar compared to men, and

3 Katherine Schaeffer, "6 facts about economic inequality in the U.S.," Pew Research Center, February 7, 2020, https://www.pewresearch.org/fact-tank/2020/02/07/6-facts-about-economic-inequality-in-the-u-s/.

4 Ana Hernández Kent and Lowell Ricketts, "Has Wealth Inequality in America Changed over Time? Here Are Key Statistics," Federal Reserve Bank of St. Louis, December 2, 2020, https://www.stlouisfed.org/open-vault/2020/december/has-wealth-inequality-changed-over-time-key-statistics#authorbox.

the gap is wider for women of color.[5] Because of this pay gap, and because women are still more likely to take time away from paid work to do care work, we also still see a wealth gap between men and women.[6] Taking time away from paid work not only means lost earnings and lost savings but it also translates to lower Social Security payments in the future.

This wealth gap is particularly important because women live longer than men, on average, and retire earlier than men, on average. The typical woman actually needs to save *more* than the typical man in order to maintain her standard of living in retirement.

There is some evidence that younger women are making the effort to change their financial futures. Women under fifty-five are more than four times as likely as older women to say they are knowledgeable about financial matters—in fact, women under thirty-five actually score better on financial literacy quizzes than their male peers.[7] The face of wealth is starting to change too. Women around the world are growing their financial assets 1.5 times faster than men, and by 2025 women are expected to control about 35 percent of global financial assets.

Despite this progress, the wealth gaps between women and

---

5 Robin Bleiweis, "Quick Facts About the Gender Wage Gap," Center for American Progress, March 24, 2020, https://www.americanprogress.org/article/quick-facts-gender-wage-gap/.

6 Reshma Kapadia, "The Stubborn Wealth Gap Between Men and Women," *Barron's*, April 18, 2018, https://www.barrons.com/articles/the-stubborn-wealth-gap-between-men-and-women-1524099601.

7 "Get ready for the next generation of women investors," Merrill Lynch, accessed April 12, 2022, https://www.ml.com/articles/get-ready-for-the-next-generation-of-women-investors.html.

men, and white people and people of color, persist. These wealth gaps are a tragedy. It's not just about dollars and cents. I often say I'm in the peace-of-mind business because that's what I do for my clients. I help them achieve that peace of mind that comes from knowing you're not so vulnerable to the ordinary twists and turns of life.

Women and people of color need good financial planning advice. Women and people of color deserve that peace of mind. But when women and people of color look at the financial advisory business, they don't see people who look like them. They might feel that the old white guys who still make up most of the industry won't really listen to them or won't understand their goals and concerns. The lack of diversity in the industry becomes a vicious cycle that perpetuates mistrust and misunderstanding.

But that vicious cycle can become a virtuous one if more women and people of color enter the industry. LeCount Davis, the first Black man to become a Certified Financial Planner in the United States, has said that he owes his success to the fact that he built a mostly Black client base.[8] He reached out to people like him, people who were underserved by the advisory business and who had an urgent need for good financial advice. And he built a great career.

That's one reason why I believe there's a world of opportunity in this industry for women and minorities: there's a huge untapped market of people who need good advice but who right now don't see a lot of advisors who they can relate to. Of course, diverse advisors

8 Jason Bisnoff, "Diversity In Wealth Management Still 'Awful,' Advisors Say," *Forbes*, October 13, 2020, https://www.forbes.com/sites/jasonbisnoff/2020/10/13/diversity-in-wealth-management-still-awful-advisors-say/?sh=3991278d4494.

shouldn't feel restricted to working only with clients who look like them but serving these underserved populations could be one way to start building a thriving business.

An Aging Industry

The wealth management field isn't just pale and male. It's also going gray. The average advisor today is fifty-five years old, and about 20 percent of advisors are over sixty-five.[9] Only 11 percent of advisors are under forty.

This also spells opportunity. At least 20 percent of advisors will probably be retiring within the next ten to fifteen years. Think how much space that opens up in the industry! Many of those aging advisors' clients are probably younger than they are—and new potential clients are opening their first 401(k)s and IRAs every day.

Like women and people of color, younger adults also urgently need good financial planning advice. As of 2020, millennials—young adults ages 25–40—owned only 4.6 percent of the total wealth in the United States. Baby boomers own 53 percent, and Gen X owns 25 percent[10]. It's natural for older people to be wealthier than younger people, as they've had more time to earn and accumulate assets. And boomer parents are expected to pass

9 "Technology, Social Media Critical to Bridging Financial Advisor Age Gap, J. D. Power Finds," J. D. Power, accessed April 12, 2022, https://www.jdpower.com/business/press-releases/2019-us-financial-advisor-satisfaction-study.

10 Alicia Adamczyk, "Millennials own less than 5% of all U.S. wealth," CNBC, October 9, 2020, https://www.cnbc.com/2020/10/09/millennials-own-less-than-5percent-of-all-us-wealth.html.

down trillions of dollars in wealth to their millennial kids in the coming decades. But millennials are far behind where their boomer parents were when they were their age. When boomers were the age millennials are now, they owned 21 percent of the total wealth in the country. Millennials also hold more of their wealth in real estate than any other generation, meaning their wealth is concentrated in a slower-growth asset—compared to equities, for example.[11]

A young adult who's between the ages of twenty-five and forty has time to grow their assets and prepare for retirement. But they'll need good advice to do that effectively. And they'll definitely need good financial advice if and when they inherit money from their boomer parents. Younger adults also might prefer to work with younger advisors who they can relate to—and who they can rely on to stay in business throughout their peak earning years.

For all these reasons, I believe there's a world of opportunity in the financial advisory business, particularly for young women and young people of color. For example, there are 331 million individual people with assets between $100,000 and $3 million.[12] This "surging middle class" needs financial planning advice, and many wealth management firms still focus too narrowly on the ultrawealthy.

The wealth management business doesn't look like America right now, and it should. This is as much about expanding opportunities as it is about social justice. Up until now, the advisory

11 Omri Wallach, "Charting The Growing Generational Wealth Gap," Visual Capitalist, December 2, 2020, https://www.visualcapitalist.com/charting-the-growing-generational-wealth-gap/.

12 Abby Schultz, "Total Global Wealth Rose to US$431 Trillion in 2020," *Barron's*, June 10, 2021, https://www.barrons.com/articles/total-global-wealth-rose-to-us-431-trillion-in-2020-01623322810?st=fcxxqwxnutcyrh8.

business has been poorly understood, and I think that's held back a lot of people. If you want to be a doctor, you pretty much know what it takes to get there. The same isn't true for advisors.

For the right person—a person who is entrepreneurial, loves people, and wants to build a business from the ground up—this is one of the best and most exciting professions to be in. As an advisor, you're your own boss. There's no ceiling on your income.

Of course, being your own boss also means that your success or failure is almost entirely up to you. You can and should look for mentors and supporters in the industry and find opportunities to team up with colleagues. But ultimately, building your business is all up to you.

Remember: you don't need to come into the business with connections to wealthy people to be successful. I certainly didn't.

Beginning with Rejection

I was rejected the first time I applied to work as a broker. I had two master's degrees—an MBA and a master's in communications—but I was told I didn't have what it would take to succeed.

First of all, I didn't have the contacts. Back then, the business still operated with a country-club mentality. The first firm I interviewed with clearly expected me to come in knowing a lot of wealthy prospective clients. The manager literally told me, "Raj, you seem like a good guy, but without any contacts you won't succeed in this business." Another manager asked me if I belonged to a country club where I could prospect. I told him I did not play golf, because it was an expensive hobby. At the time, the richest person I knew was my mother, who had $20,000 in a 401(k).

They also put me through a couple of tests. The first was basically a test of endurance. They put me in a room with two phones. About every five minutes, someone called and told me to buy and sell stocks as a mock exercise. I stayed calm and collected throughout.

I passed that test, but I flunked the psych test they gave me next. I think the disconnect might have been cultural. On an American résumé, it's not uncommon to say things like, "I turned around IBM." Americans tend to be very individualistic. In India, if you said that, you'd sound like a jerk. Work in India is much more focused on the team.

Every answer I gave on that test focused on teamwork and collaboration. Incidentally, that's the spirit in which I run my business today. But thirty years ago, there really was no teamwork in the business. That collaborative spirit got me rejected.

The person who interviewed me said, "Raj, we're looking for people who can pull their socks up and grind it out." They just didn't see that in me.

An Accidental Advisor

I came from a middle-class Indian family, and education was a big priority. My dad was a pharmaceutical chemist, my grandfather was a lawyer, and my maternal grandfather was an engineer. We were far from wealthy, but we never lacked for education.

My dad had told me that I should get an MBA. He said there was a future in banking. Of course, I didn't listen—at first. I was focused on breaking into radio. From age eighteen to twenty-four, I worked at an English-language radio station in Hyderabad, in South India. It was one of only two stations in the city, and it was the station for young people. The show was live—I took requests, talked, and played Western music. Honestly, it was a great job. I'd drive my motorbike around the city, and people would recognize me. I thought I was going to be in radio for my entire life.

But dads are usually right—with about a twenty-year lag. I wasn't paid much as a radio DJ, so I'd gotten a degree in economics and a day job selling green stamps to retailers. Green stamps were one of the earliest retail loyalty programs. After a while, I moved over to a competitor, and then I got my MBA.

At twenty-four, I came to the United States to get a master's in communications at Emerson. I worked in media until 1987, producing documentaries and commercials, doing creative work on the side. I enjoyed it. I loved the people I worked with, but I was tired of jumping from project to project. I wanted to build something that would last.

I fell into the advisory business by accident. I met with my stockbroker—that's what they were called in the eighties—to liquidate a brokerage account to buy a condo. I told this guy I was thinking of changing careers, and he said he thought I'd do great in his business.

Obviously, the first firm I applied to didn't think so. But I kept going. I went out for more interviews. Six months after my first interview, I got a call from a headhunter that Merrill was looking to speak with me. A gentleman named Bob Spangler interviewed me and hired me on the spot. That was one of the best days of my life, and I am eternally grateful to Bob and Merrill Lynch for giving me a break. Everyone needs someone to give them a start, and Bob gave me mine.

A few years later, I was asked to speak to a large conference of financial advisors in Woodstock, Vermont, on my success in the business. By this time, I was in the top 5 percent of my training class. The manager who invited me was the same one who rejected me from my first interview. He didn't remember, but I did. We shared a laugh, and to this day he is a good friend.

I had terrible timing. I joined the wealth management business in 1987, just before the Black Monday crash. As the new guy in the office, I was put to work answering phones for the senior brokers. Once the crash hit in October, clients were calling all day, panicking. There was almost no financial media at the time, and certainly no 24-7 cable channels. People would call just to get quotes. The senior brokers weren't reaching out to them proactively to talk about what was happening—they were freaking out.

As the new guy, I was also working hard to try to build a business. I would cold-call people, because that was how it was done back then, and find that they just wanted someone to talk to. That's when I began to learn the importance of communication. People desperately wanted to hear from an expert—to get some reassurance that market slides were normal.

Swimming Upstream

I was miserable trying to build a business by cold-calling. And I didn't know a lot of rich people to jump-start my business. So how did I get started? If you are just starting out in the business, are you doomed to spend your days cold-calling strangers?

In case it's not already clear, the answer is no. I found another way, and so can you.

My journey to success really began when I started doing some market segmentation research on potential clients in the Boston area. This was before the tech revolution, so my research revealed that the people who had money in the area were mainly doctors. Anecdotally, I was noticing the same thing: when I went to parties, all the people pulling up in Mercedes were doctors.

Luckily for me, I had a lot of doctors in my family, so I felt like I could relate to them. I worked up a pitch for retirement planning that was tailored to doctors' concerns. And then I walked into Mass General and asked to see their HR department.

I told the office manager that I wanted to do a free seminar on retirement planning for their staff. She said they were all set. But I didn't let that stop me. I sent their head of HR a note every single week. After a few weeks, I went back to the office, waited until the receptionist went on a break, and made it in to see the boss.

The HR head at the hospital agreed to let me give a seminar, as long as I served lunch. *My* boss said I had to pay for the lunch myself. So my first big investment in business development was forty sandwiches from Au Bon Pain.

Twenty-five people showed up for that first lunch, and they left five minutes later, sandwiches in hand. My next key business lesson: serve lunch at the end!

It didn't seem like an auspicious beginning. But I ended up getting my first clients from that seminar. From there, I earned referrals and built my business through networking.

Conventional wisdom told me the only way to build my business was by cold-calling random strangers and pushing them to sell stocks and bonds. But I knew in my gut that approach wasn't right for me.

Cold-calling might have been the best way to build the kind of business that everybody else had at the time. But I didn't want to build that kind of business. I wanted to build a business that felt authentic to who I was—a conservative, long-term investor, not a trader; a natural connector and communicator, not a salesperson.

Especially if you're young, a woman, or a person of color, the business you want to build might not look like the average wealth management business today. But that can be a strength. As the world changes, there's a huge opportunity in creating businesses that better reflect the communities and cultures we serve. If you stay true to who you are and build a business that feels authentic to who you are, there's a world of opportunity for you in this industry.

Key Takeaways

- The dominance of white males in the industry reflects the wealth gap in society; we need more financial advisors who reflect the population in order to reach a more diverse client base.
- I was turned down by several firms when I applied for a job in the industry. Merrill Lynch took a chance on me in August 1987, two months prior to the Black Monday market crash of 1987.
- I was expected to cold-call for clients. It was not an approach I embraced; I preferred the seminar and networking route. It wasn't until I started giving informational seminars to doctors that I started getting clients.

3

PURPOSE AND DIRECTION

I remember meeting an incredibly smart kid from another major Wall Street firm about twenty years ago. He was just getting into the business and was looking for advice. I asked him why he'd joined the business. He'd previously worked as a headhunter, so this was a pretty big career change for him.

His answer: "I heard there's a lot of money to be made."

"Sure," I said, "but that's true of a lot of fields. You can be successful in a lot of different fields."

"This is faster," he said. "You don't have to sell anything—it's all on paper."

Fast-forward ten years, and he was marched out of his office by regulators and barred from the business forever. He'd been churning—buying and selling stocks at a rapid rate in order to generate commissions—his clients' accounts.

He came into this business with the wrong mindset. All he cared about was making money. It's not surprising that he ended up doing whatever it took to get ahead.

I certainly wouldn't have hired that guy for my team. He did well for a while. He was persuasive and had no trouble signing people up as clients. The sad truth is, he had everything he needed to succeed for the long term. But he couldn't sustain his success. He was so focused on short-term gains that he couldn't even see the long-term consequences of his actions.

Purpose Is What Sustains You

I joined Merrill at the age of thirty-one. I'd already been through several careers—a radio DJ, consumer marketer, management executive, filmmaker, and media professional. Although I excelled in most of my jobs, I never felt fulfilled. I was searching for something more, a career in which I could control my destiny, my time, and my financial rewards.

As an advisor, you are an *entrepreneur* in the truest sense of the word. Nobody hands you clients on a gilt-edged platter—you must convert prospects into clients and build a team that can serve your clients effectively to accomplish their goals and dreams.

There's enormous satisfaction and opportunity in controlling your own destiny. You can be as ambitious as you want. No one places a ceiling on your income potential. It is based on your ability to gather assets and retain clients.

But if your only reason for joining the wealth management business is to make money, you have chosen the wrong career. Doing well for yourself is a by-product of serving your clients and enhancing their lives. Don't get me wrong—the job of an advisor is financially rewarding, but that by itself cannot be your reason for getting into this business.

Not only does a narrow focus on money alone leave you vulnerable to taking ethical shortcuts, like that young man I met, but it's ultimately unrewarding. Nobody ends up on their deathbed thinking, *If only I'd made another million dollars*! Making money might motivate you for a while, but eventually financial rewards alone will feel hollow. Research has actually proven money doesn't buy you happiness. Higher salaries improve people's emotional well-being, but only up to $75,000. Beyond that point, money can improve your intellectual evaluation of your level of success, but not your emotional experience. To keep going in this business for the long haul, you need to be motivated by a purpose greater than money.

I wake up every morning with a sense of optimism. I know full well I can't control the economy or the markets. But I know I can influence my own attitude, work ethic, and determination. I can control the way I communicate with clients and how proactive I am about educating them in my approach to investing and reaching out when markets slide. And I can control the amount of time I devote to educating myself. I'm always learning about a new aspect of the business; a new area of opportunity; or economic, political, and demographic trends around the world. My clients trust our team because of our knowledge and competence, our ability to navigate markets, our experience, and our track record in developing clear financial plans and strategies for success.

I couldn't work as hard as I do just to make money. If I were just in it for the money, I would have retired by now. What keeps me going is my purpose—my desire to help my clients achieve their dreams.

In order to sustain any endeavor, you have to be driven by a larger purpose. If you aren't, you'll be one of the many casualties who quits the business after just a few years. I've seen far too many people in this business who've failed, not because they're not smart, or they don't have the right degrees, or they don't know how to build a balanced portfolio, but because they could not or did not define their *purpose* for being in this business.

The average person spends ninety thousand hours—a third of their life—at work. What remains of all that time when you're gone? Your legacy. How did you touch people? How did you elevate the people around you? In the end, that's all that matters.

I'm not saying we all have to be Mahatma Gandhi. But we can all think about the contribution we want to make to the world. We can all think about whether the work we're doing, in some way, leaves the world a better place.

Purpose Drives Everything You Do

The great Indian poet Rabindranath Tagore wrote: "I slept and dreamt that life was joy. I awoke and saw that life was service. I acted and behold, service was joy."

Today I live by those words. But my sense of purpose didn't come to me on day one. It evolved over time. It might take you years, even decades, to understand your own purpose, but reflecting on your purpose is always a worthwhile endeavor.

I evolved my sense of purpose in part by learning from mentors. One of my mentors was Augie Cenname, who to this day is a wonderful wealth advisor with Merrill Lynch. He had already built a strong team by the early eighties, so he was well established when I was just joining the business. He was incredibly successful, yet so humble. I took every opportunity I could to talk to him and to learn more about how he worked. It was always clear how much he cared about his clients. Everything he did was client centric. He always put their needs first.

I learned a lot from people like Augie. Even though I didn't have a clear sense of my purpose when I first started in the business, I had a gut sense of what felt right to me. I always knew I wouldn't be able to live with myself if I built a business by pushing clients to trade a lot. I always knew I wanted to build a sustainable, client-first business, even if it meant giving up some short-term gains.

That was the beginning of the evolution of my sense of purpose—a gut sense that I had to put clients' needs first. What matters most to you? Maybe you're driven by a desire to work for social justice by helping people who have too long been shut out of the world of wealth. Maybe you see yourself as a role model to other young people in your community. Maybe you're passionate about the environment, and you want to help spread the word about sustainable investing. Maybe your purpose will evolve out of a simple desire to provide a stable, comfortable life for your family. Money matters to all of us, but you have to look beyond money to start to discover your bigger purpose.

When you know your big why, you have a framework for what you're doing. From there, you can fill in the details. I'm on the board of a nonprofit called the American India Foundation, and I often ask my fellow board members, "Why are we doing what we're doing?" In that case, our purpose is to disrupt poverty in India. Keeping that purpose in mind helps guide the details of what we choose to do and not to do. Starting from that broad purpose, we can start filling in the framework with questions like: What are the dimensions of poverty? What are our strategies for addressing the problem? If we were thinking of funding an education initiative, for example, we'd have to ask ourselves how educating this population will disrupt poverty. Everything should tie back to the mission.

The same goes for my business. Today, after decades of reflection, my sense of purpose drives everything I do and everything my team does. Our purpose is to make a difference in our clients' lives and to help them achieve their most cherished dreams and goals. Everything we do should serve that purpose. It's not just an empty slogan; it's the framework for my business plan. It determines my business goals, changes who I hire, and ultimately touches every aspect of my business. I'm sure my team gets sick of hearing me talk about this stuff, but I talk about our mission, purpose, and values on every call we have as a team. Our strategies and tactics flow from that purpose.

I believe in the power of purpose so much that I've begun integrating this idea into my work with clients. These days many of my clients are quite wealthy. In the past five or six years, I've started asking them: Have you thought about the purpose of your wealth?

Most answer honestly that they haven't.

I love opening up this conversation with clients because it leads them in such interesting directions. Most people's first impulse is to say their purpose is to take care of their family. And certainly, when I was first starting out, most of my clients were focused on these bread-and-butter issues. But these days many of my clients have more than enough money to take care of their families and still have a substantial amount left over. Once we start talking about the question of purpose, clients will often start to think about philanthropy. They'll make a comment like, "I've always wanted to do something for wildlife," and that simple thought can be the beginning of a journey that ends in the creation of a foundation to protect wildlife around the world.

Even when my clients don't bring philanthropy up themselves,

I often raise it with them. Why? I believe philanthropy is a way to bring a family together around a common purpose. My goal is to make a difference in my clients' lives, and the biggest difference I could make is to help them unlock the greater level of satisfaction that comes from having a deeper purpose.

Mark Twain once said, "The two most important days of your life are the day you were born and the day you find out why."

This is easier said than done. It may take years or even decades to find your true purpose, and it also changes over time. But I believe there's no more important question to ask than *why*. Purpose is the reason for your existence and the "why" of your life. Everything flows from there: Your purpose articulates why you do what you do, your vision is your big-picture goal of where you want to go, and your mission is designed to motivate you to get there. Finding purpose is a prerequisite for happiness and fulfillment.

Simply asking the question, "What is my purpose?" can be the beginning of an immensely enriching journey that will add great meaning to your life.

Digging into the Details

Once you understand your bigger purpose, you can start to chart your specific course and set goals that will help you achieve that purpose. If you're just starting out in the business, you'll need not only a purpose but a direction—clear, actionable goals that will guide you through beginning a career.

When I started in the business, there were only two main roles: financial advisor and client associate. Today the opportunity set has broadened substantially. Depending on your skills, interest, and aptitude, you can now be an investment analyst, relationship manager, wealth strategist, business manager, and several other new roles, based on the business focus of the team. This is a huge field, and there are lots of different roles built to suit different strengths and personalities. Keep in mind that this is a highly regulated industry—as it should be! Any role will require certain exams and certifications and come with legal responsibilities. You should do your own research to determine which areas of the field you're most interested in, but let's briefly walk through a few main options.

Financial planner: Financial planners create holistic plans for their clients' financial lives. You need to be a good listener and a good communicator—you'll often need to read between the lines to understand what truly matters to your client and how to help them prepare for the biggest moments in their lives.

Relationship manager: Relationship managers work under the guidance of a financial advisor. Their job is to ensure that proper financial plans are created and maintained. They also play a key role in rebalancing portfolios according to client goals, time horizon, and risk tolerance. Working alongside the financial advisor, relationship managers are critical to managing, cultivating, and deepening client relationships.

Wealth management advisor, also called financial advisor: Wealth advisors work with high-net-worth individuals, families, and endowments to create comprehensive financial plans and develop appropriate investment strategies. A crucial aspect of this role is prospecting, making presentations, and developing new business. In short, to be an effective wealth management advisor, you need to be a rainmaker. Your ability to build, inspire, and lead a team is also an essential prerequisite for success. Your team is the symphony; you are the conductor. From developing processes for service to investment strategy, your vision and leadership will shape the team's ethos. As a leader, your role is to help develop the talents and careers of every single member. It's an incredibly entrepreneurial challenge. I have always viewed myself as running a boutique growth company within a large firm.

Client service officer: This is a key support role, so you'd be doing a little bit of everything. You'd prepare plans and review progress to help your advisor get ready for client meetings, and you'd help ensure that clients get regular communication from the office. You'd also play a crucial role in the administrative process of a client relationship. You'll need a good head for details and the ability to work in close coordination with the primary financial advisor and relationship manager to ensure that all the clients' needs are being met. The success of a client relationship is in large part due to the close coordination between the advisor and client services officer. No matter how good your team's financial performance may be, if you fail on the service side, you may end up losing your client.

Analyst: These are the number crunchers who analyze investment options and provide research to advisors. It's a behind-the-scenes role, so your math skills and your ability to read a balance sheet and income statement are typically more important than prospecting.

In addition to the above, there may be roles in larger teams for a business manager, wealth strategist, or general administrative roles, such as travel, entertainment, and scheduling. An emerging new role on teams is a family dynamics coordinator. In this role, you will help families clarify and define the mission and purpose of their wealth and define their long-term legacy.

These aren't the only options, of course. But if you're just starting out in the advisory business, you should think carefully about what types of roles you might be best suited for. And even if you've been in the business for a while, it's worth looking around and reevaluating every few years. Are you happy with the type of work you're doing? Is there another role you're drawn to? Do you look at your boss or mentor and think, *I want* that *job*? Or do you want to move in a different direction?

The other key question to consider early in your career is whether to join an established firm or start a business all on your own. I found that joining Merrill Lynch was a happy medium. When I was just starting out, I could partner with more experienced advisors to try to land a big client, and I had the firm's great team of analysts to help guide my portfolio design. But I was still building my own business, ultimately succeeding or failing on my own. It was still my decision when and how to invest money back into my business and hire an assistant or bring on a new advisor.

Of course, you can always go it completely alone—get a CFP or other certification and set up your own shop, unaffiliated with any larger firm. Or you can start in client services or another support role and try to learn the ropes before you begin building your own business. Ultimately, you have to know yourself in order to know where you'll fit best.

Key Takeaways

- To succeed in wealth management, you must realize it is about more than making money.

- You must have a larger purpose for what you do. For me, it is serving my customers and bringing them peace of mind.

- Once you know your purpose, you can set your goals accordingly.
- There are a number of roles in the industry today beyond financial advisor and client associate, the only two when my career began.
- Today you can become a financial planner, a relationship advisor, a wealth management advisor, a client service officer, an analyst, and various other roles within the financial management world.

4

BUSINESS PHILOSOPHY

People don't buy what you do; they buy why you do it.
—Simon Sinek

I followed my own instincts when I started my business. Everyone told me to get clients by cold-calling strangers and convincing them to buy stocks. I hated doing that, so I found another approach: I targeted doctors and started providing free educational seminars to introduce myself to potential clients. In the end, this method worked—and it was a method I could live with.

You can't build a business doing something you hate. It's not sustainable. If you want long-term success, your business must be grounded in philosophies and strategies that feel authentic to your personality.

I got into the business at the tail end of the era of commissions, so initially the only way I could make a living was on commissions, trade by trade. You'd call up your clients and say, "Such-and-so bond is being offered. I think it might be appropriate for your portfolio. To be transparent, I'll be paid five hundred dollars for this transaction. Is that OK with you?" If they agreed, you'd make the trade and get paid.

The problem with this approach was that doing nothing meant you didn't get paid. And when it comes to investing, doing nothing is often the right thing to do. If a stock doesn't need to be sold, why sell it?

This was an ethical dilemma for me from day one. That's why I was so eager to embrace the asset-based method of charging my clients. That change was a moment of liberation for me in this business. I applaud Merrill Lynch for being a trailblazer in the asset-based pricing movement.

The Dawn of Financial Planning

Even when I was working on commission, I was interested in the idea of financial planning. I'd learned from my previous corporate jobs to always think about objectives. I strongly believe if you don't know where you're going, you'll never get there. So, even as a commission-based advisor, I'd ask my clients about their long-term goals and what they hoped to accomplish with their investments. Under the old model, I didn't technically need to know this information, but I always found it helped orient me to who my clients were and helped me find that sense of purpose that's always been important to me.

If you don't know your clients' goals, every client is the same. Every account is just a string of numbers, and you're trying to make the numbers go up. To me, it's much more meaningful and motivating to get to know my clients. That way, each account becomes a story. I'm not just trying to make the numbers grow; I'm trying to help Julie provide for her family or help Andrew fund that wildlife organization he's so passionate about.

I eagerly embraced the shift to asset-based pricing in the early 1990s. And I began to embrace the financial planning methodology even before Merrill Lynch introduced formal financial planning as an option. Today financial planning is the foundation of everything I do and everything Merrill Lynch advisors do. Every client relationship begins with an extensive questionnaire about goals, lifestyle, and risk tolerance. This model not only feels more authentic to me but it has led me to develop my business philosophy.

My Holistic Approach

If your purpose is your North Star, then your business philosophy is the map to your destination. It's the details of *how* you're going to achieve that big *why*.

My purpose is to help my clients achieve their dreams.

My business philosophy is one of holistic financial planning.

I believe this is the best way to achieve my purpose: to approach each client as an individual with unique hopes and dreams and to work on all aspects of their financial life, not just their investments.

That means I do a lot of work on my clients' behalf that I don't technically get paid for. My clients come to my team for help with anything and everything that affects them. I often help clients network, connecting them with lawyers or potential investors for their businesses. I've even helped clients find doctors.

And that's the secret to the success of my holistic philosophy:

my team's wraparound services build incredible long-lasting client loyalty. Of course, our strong investment results help. But ultimately, a lot of financial planners out there could help my clients grow their assets. What they can't get anywhere else is an advisor who is truly devoted to helping them with every challenge they face.

My Philosophy in Practice

I developed this approach early in my career. Once I moved into asset-based pricing and formal financial planning, I started offering additional services, like tax and estate planning strategy. My team was very early in offering estate and legacy planning strategy, for example. That's another service I don't get paid for—the attorney gets paid, but I don't. After all, the attorneys are the only ones who can draft a legal document. I offer estate planning advice because I want to help my clients achieve their goals, and those goals often include providing for their children and making philanthropic contributions. Helping them prepare their wills helps them ensure that their legacy will be in line with their goals.

Some advisors might view services like tax or estate planning strategy as loss leaders. I call them profit leaders. These kinds of services are the foundation of my relationships with my clients. My clients trust me because they know I'm looking out for their interests more than I am for my own bottom line. Luckily, that lifetime trust ultimately benefits my bottom line too.

Here are just a few of the non-investment-related services I've provided for my clients:

Introducing children to investing. With my own kids, their eyes glaze over when I try to talk to them about investments. I probably talked about finance too much when they were young. But these days lots of my clients ask me to help their children learn the basics of putting together a portfolio.

Prenups. This has been coming up more and more as my longtime clients are getting older, and their kids are getting to be marriage age. I'll meet with my client, my client's child, and an estate planner and strategist to talk about how to protect the family's assets. I've even talked to a client's child's fiancé on the family's behalf.

Elder care concerns. Sometimes my clients' children come to me with worries about their parents' memory and mental state. We will facilitate a conversation for the family and help them work with an attorney to transfer power of attorney to the children so they can ensure their parents are taken care of.

Philanthropy. As more and more of my clients get involved in philanthropy, this is something my team has been doing more often. Creating a family foundation or a donor-advised fund to support a specific philanthropic goal is an option that we'll talk about with clients, and if they're interested, we'll connect them with the attorneys and other experts they need to work with.

Business challenges. I built my own business from scratch, and many of my clients are entrepreneurs and business leaders. I'm always happy to take a call from a client who has a business problem, whether it's a dispute with a start-up cofounder or a marketing challenge. My job is to offer them my perspectives and insights as a businessperson.

Creating custom solutions. Recently, a client wanted to help her daughter buy a condo. But she wanted her daughter to put some money up, too, so she had to take some responsibility. We talked to a CPA about tax implications and brought in an attorney who created a customized agreement that enabled the client to give her daughter a portion of the cost and essentially write a mortgage loan for the balance. I'm always happy to brainstorm creative ideas with clients to accomplish their desired outcomes.

I'm always willing to go the extra mile for my clients. Loyalty is a two-way street—I stick with my clients no matter what, even as I hope they'll stick with me. One of my clients was overwhelmed with stress when the pandemic hit. He's a supersmart, high-achieving guy, but he had recently lost his spouse, and he was living on his own. I knew he was struggling to cope. My team referred him to Merrill Lynch's Family Office group, which now helps him with bill payment, tracking his net worth, and managing his real estate, as well as setting up a regular grocery delivery schedule. He didn't have any family to help him, so our family office stepped up and played that role.

Holistic Doesn't Mean Anything Goes

Of course, there are some requests I simply can't honor. I've had parents ask me to share what their kids are doing with their investments. I can't do that—both legally and ethically, I'm bound by client confidentiality.

Another bright line is insider trading. I've trained my team to keep an eye out for this issue. When you work with high-powered, connected clients, it does come up. Clients don't mean to skirt ethical rules, but we have to watch out for them. If a client comes to us and says we've got to buy *X* stock, I have to ask, "How did you hear about this?" The information must come from a public source—it can't be something a friend shared over drinks.

You always have to be willing to push back on clients, no matter how long they've been with you. Ethics come first.

Minimums Are a Must

My holistic approach makes mine a very high-touch business. It'd be impossible for me to scale this up and do this type of extensive support for a thousand families.

Raising my minimums was a pivot point for me. It sparked dramatic growth in my business. I'd been in business for a few years, and I'd gotten very good at opening accounts. I'd go over to Mass General and open seventeen new accounts in a week. At one point I probably had almost four hundred clients. But it was taking a toll on me. The stress was becoming overwhelming. I'd go out to grab a sandwich for lunch, and when I got back twenty minutes later I'd already have six messages waiting for me on those little "while you were out" notes. The receptionist was getting worried about me.

I was struggling to keep up. I couldn't return calls as quickly as I wanted. I knew I had to do something, and the obvious answer was to raise my minimums.

I started by raising my minimum to $1 million. Eventually, I went to $2.5 million, then $5 million, and today my minimum is $10 million. I'll still take on smaller accounts if I meet someone who has a lot of potential, or if I get a referral from a friend or client. But raising my minimums has allowed me to limit my business to about one hundred core households. Given my holistic approach and my willingness to do whatever it takes to make sure my clients can achieve their goals, this is a workable size for my practice. When people who don't meet my minimums reach out to me, I refer them to a network of advisors we've collaborated with for over a decade. We understand their style, client service process, investment philosophy, and importantly, their ethics and transparency.

Not every practice needs to have minimums in the multimillions. Some advisors are drawn to work with younger clients, or clients with smaller nest eggs. Your business doesn't have to look like mine or anybody else's—you need to find your own philosophy. Just like finding your purpose, this can be a process. My business philosophy, my holistic approach to wealth management, has evolved over time.

Finding Your Investment Philosophy

Part of creating your business philosophy is developing your investment philosophy. Of course, you'll customize each client's financial plan to their specific goals, style, and needs. But you should come into every new client relationship with your own approach. You can't be all things to all people. You must have your own style, and you have to be willing to turn away clients who aren't interested in what you're offering.

My approach is one of responsible asset management. I'm not in the speculation game, and I'm not in the trading game. I build very diversified portfolios because I believe that's the best and safest way to accumulate wealth over time.

I customize my investment approach to every client's needs, of course. I give every client a fifty-question risk tolerance questionnaire, with plenty of trick questions to catch those people who think they're comfortable taking on significant risk but can't handle losses. Even very sophisticated people will sometimes say they're hoping for a 20 percent return on the upside but can only stomach a 5 percent drop on the downside! As an advisor, educating clients about market history, fluctuations, and drawdowns is an absolute must prior to taking on a new relationship. Markets are wonderful over the long term, but over any short-term period the fluctuations can be unnerving.

I've refused a lot of business. That potential client who wants a 20 percent return with no downside risk—if they're not willing to be educated about what's realistic, you will get into trouble with that client. I also turn down potential clients who are interested in trading options and other more speculative strategies. There are other advisors who will take those accounts, who are comfortable with a more active, trading-based approach. That's simply not my style, and I won't be a good fit with someone who's interested in that type of investing. We'll discuss this more in chapter 7.

Developing Your Own Philosophy

Remember: your business and investment philosophies can evolve over time. Today I have a very clear sense of who I am, what kind of advisor I am, and what kind of clients I want to work with. When I was first starting out, I couldn't have articulated all of this so easily. And I took on almost any client who would have me for those first few years.

To develop your own business philosophy, as you begin to build a stable of clients, pay attention to who you enjoy working with the most and why. Think about the aspects of your work that you find most rewarding. Take time at least once a year to reflect on what you've accomplished in the past year and think about where you want your business to go. Ask yourself:

- Who is my ideal client?
- What work am I doing now that I'd like to be doing more often?
- What work would I like to be doing less frequently?
- In an ideal world, what additional services would I like to offer my clients?

Continually reflecting and refining your approach in this way will help you hone in on a business philosophy that will sustain your interest and excitement over the long haul.

To develop your investment philosophy, start with your own instincts as an investor. Sit down and take the risk questionnaire that you give to new clients. Trying to manage investments for clients who are way outside your personal comfort zone is a recipe for stress. It's always worth stretching yourself and learning about new asset classes, but if you know in your gut that, like me, you'll never be an options trader, you shouldn't try to trade options for your clients.

Your approach to managing money on behalf of your clients can and will evolve as you learn more about the business and gain more experience. But you should always stay grounded in what feels authentic to who you are. I'm a cautious, long-term investor who prioritizes peace of mind for myself and my clients. I've built an incredible business by staying true to who I am—and you can too.

Key Takeaways

- Once you know your business purpose, then you can determine how to carry out that purpose. This is your business philosophy.
- My business philosophy is all about holistic financial planning.
- In practice, this means providing many wraparound services in addition to the financial planning basics. This encompasses estate, tax, legacy, and philanthropic strategies. My team also tracks client net worth, focusing on both assets and liabilities.
- I offer financial advice to my clients' children and help them think through issues such as prenups and budgeting.
- My team has minimum asset criteria for clients and will turn down clients who intend to pursue speculative forms of financial investing.
- Each financial advisor must develop their own criteria and business philosophy based on their purpose.

5

ESTABLISHING A UNIQUE BRAND

It takes twenty years to build a reputation and five minutes to ruin it. If you think about that, you'll do things differently.
—Warren Buffett

Differentiation is the key to success in any type of business. The world of wealth management is a crowded space, with literally thousands of service providers. Everyone from discount brokerages to local banks to insurance companies to major Wall Street firms is competing for your clients' attention.

How do you stand out in this vast space?

I always come back to purpose. Purpose is the North Star that shapes your identity. I strongly believe this business should be about more than making money.

Your unique brand starts with your purpose. But it doesn't end there. To build a unique brand, you'll also need to find a niche within the market.

Your Own Place in the World

Finding a niche is a great way to focus your brand and your business development activities. If your target clients are "people with money," where do you spend your marketing dollars? Narrowing down your target market can really help you figure out where to find clients.

For years, I've found a very rewarding niche in working with entrepreneurs and corporate executives—in other words, wealth creators. About 80 percent of the money we manage is first-generation wealth. Most of our clients are people who didn't start out wealthy but who have achieved enormous success throughout their lifetimes and need to figure out how to manage this change in their lives in a sustainable, healthy way.

Your niche might be people from your community, people your age, or people in a certain profession you feel drawn to. Or you might focus on cash flow planning in retirement, financial planning for young parents, anything that calls to you.

Once you've identified your niche, you must work to understand their unique needs. That's something my team and I have devoted a lot of time to over the years—understanding our clients' specific needs holistically. For example, a lot of our clients have a large portion of their wealth tied up in one stock, either from a company they've founded or a company they've worked in for many years. They need help diversifying their wealth over time. Estate planning under these conditions also comes with some unique challenges. If the company in question is privately held, and the stock isn't liquid, the client might need additional insurance, such as key man insurance, to protect their wealth.

Whatever your unique niche is, study your target clients carefully. Learn about their unique needs and challenges. Become an expert on your little corner of the world.

Remember: your brand can evolve over time too. You don't have to identify your target niche on the first day you hang your shingle. I began building my business by targeting doctors. I'd identified them as a group of people likely to have enough money to need and want help managing it.

I still like doctors, but today the core of my practice is those wealth-creating business leaders I discussed. That shift began to happen in the mid-1990s. I saw that there was a revolution happening in compensation management. Companies were starting to give stock options to rank-and-file employees, not just their top executives.

I realized there was going to be a lot of wealth created due to this shift. But stock options are complicated tax-wise. There are incentive options, nonqualified options—it's tough for most people to understand what they're getting and what they owe. At the time, a lot of tech and biotech companies were going public in my area, as the AIDS crisis drove a lot of biotech innovation, and the early tech boom took hold.

I saw a market developing, and I jumped on it. And Merrill Lynch has always been very supportive. Early on, they gave me tools and training to help me develop my expertise in stock options. That support was invaluable in helping me build up the practice I wanted to run.

Working in a Larger Firm

I've built my career while working under the Merrill Lynch umbrella. But working with a larger firm doesn't mean you don't have to do the work of branding. It's something like a surgeon, or a group of surgeons, working at a hospital. The hospital provides a lot of infrastructure and resources, including access to other specialties when the surgeon needs a consult. The surgeons can use the resources of the hospital, but they must make the decisions that are best for their patients.

Surgeons also work to build their own individual reputations. The reputation of the hospital can bring some patients through the door, but patients with specific needs will often choose a hospital based on the surgeons who practice there.

Similarly, a large firm, like Merrill Lynch, will give you some legitimacy when you're just starting out. And throughout your career, a large firm can provide useful resources and infrastructure, like that early training I got in understanding stock options. But ultimately, your individual brand is yours to build—you can't rely on the larger firm to do that work for you. It's up to you to choose your niche, identify your target market, establish your expertise, and market yourself.

Elements of a Strong Brand

Your specialization will create the core of your brand. But any wealth manager's brand needs to be supported by some key elements. These key elements include:

- Expertise and competence in all areas of financial planning. Simply put, clients will not trust you if you don't demonstrate expertise, skill, and confidence. While you can and should specialize in certain areas of financial planning, you must be competent and able to help clients with any of their financial needs.

- Investment savvy. You should always begin every client relationship by educating them about what's reasonable to expect in terms of investment returns. You should be familiar with a wide range of strategies and asset classes and be able to build strong, diversified portfolios that will succeed over the long term for your clients.

- A deep understanding of global economics. I believe a global perspective is crucial today. You need to understand the forces that drive our economic world, and to do that you can't limit yourself to focusing on one country.

- A highly qualified, competent team. Everyone on your team needs to be doing top-notch work. You set the bar high for excellence, and your entire team needs to be on the same level.

- A consultative rather than sales-oriented focus. Be patient. People hate being sold. They love being listened to.

- A client-centered approach. To be successful in your practice, the client should be the center of your universe. Focus on their success, in every dimension, and your success will follow.

My media background has certainly helped me when it comes to branding and marketing. I'm always very conscious of how we're portrayed in the media. But because word-of-mouth marketing is so important in this business, your brand starts with the work you do.

Your entire team should be aware of and engaged in the project of creating and maintaining your brand. You need to know how your team members are talking about what you do when they're meeting with clients, or even just socializing. I talk to my team about this in meetings. Sometimes we practice giving elevator pitches.

Remember: there are more than one hundred thousand advisors in the United States. The sharper you can make the distinction between your team and everyone else out there, the better. And your entire team needs to be on board in that effort.

Never Let Your Brand Go Stale

Once you've established your brand, you can't be complacent. You must constantly refresh and nourish your brand. I believe thought leadership is the best way to do this.

Establishing yourself as a thought leader means sharing information freely. Give free investment, retirement planning, or tax planning seminars to local organizations—the chamber of commerce, special interest groups, local businesses, or simply at the library. Go to local nonprofits and offer to talk to them about taxes and the markets. My team and I have established some expertise around philanthropy and changing laws, so we often go to charitable organizations and share our knowledge.

You must be sincere and driven by a desire to share information. Remember: people hate being sold, but they love being listened to. If you establish yourself as an expert, clients will come to you. You won't need the hard sell.

You want people to see you repeatedly. Think drip marketing.

Use email, LinkedIn, and other social media to strengthen your brand. Try setting up a newsletter in which you share interesting articles with clients, prospective clients, and colleagues, or jot down some thoughts on what's happening in the market.

We have a client whose father sold a biotech company. She and her husband don't work—they're classic, modest New England types, very philanthropic. The last time I met with them, I shared some thoughts about the digital economy, AI and robotics, DNA splicing and the new MRNA vaccines, and so on. Big trends that will shape the financial world—and the social and political world—for years to come. My client asked tons of questions. She was fascinated. Finally, I had to remind her that we should talk about her portfolio.

"Raj," she said, "I regularly check my accounts online. We're doing great. Can you send me some more articles on AI?"

My team's competence and skill in managing her investments are the foundation of this relationship. But it's our thought leadership around the future of the global economy that is really keeping us front of mind with this client these days.

Clients Can Be Your Best Marketers

As you build up your practice, your clients should be able to sum up your brand. They should be able to articulate what you're good at and why they stick with you. Ultimately, if you do your job well, your clients should become your marketing team. They should be out in their communities doing that all-important word-of-mouth marketing that will drive new prospective clients to check you out.

On one level, the job you're doing should speak for itself. If your clients are happy with your work, they will likely mention you to friends and will certainly pass along your name if asked for a recommendation. But you can do more to consciously prime your clients to understand and share your brand.

For example, the core of my team's brand is our holistic approach to financial planning. I am continually reinforcing this with clients in a variety of ways.

One simple thing I do is repeat the phrase, "We're in the peace-of-mind business." This is what I say when people ask me what I do, and it's something I often say to clients too. It's a simple, succinct, and compelling way to sum up my brand. By saying I'm in the "peace-of-mind business," I imply I take care of everything for my clients—and that's what I strive to do.

I have also trained my team to share with clients an eight-dimension framework for financial wellness. During client meetings, we'll refer back to this framework: "OK, we've talked about these two dimensions of wellness. How about the rest?" This helps reinforce with clients that we aren't just here to manage their investments—we care about and want to help secure all their goals.

When we have our regular check-in calls with clients, we'll also check in on their goals and ask if anything has changed. Anything is on the table, from providing for children's education to buying a vacation home to setting up a family foundation. By regularly checking in on our clients' big-picture goals, we simultaneously ensure that we're providing the services clients need, and we remind them that we take a holistic view of them. They are individuals with hopes and dreams, not numbers on a balance sheet.

My Clients Speak

Of course, the real proof of my success in getting my brand proposition across to my clients is in how they talk about me. Here are three longtime clients talking about how they see me:

- The music producer: "I met Raj before he even started in the financial advisory business, when he was working at a film and video foundation. He was the nicest guy in the world, and he was just surrounded by all these creative characters. Investing with Raj was the easiest decision in the world—I just trusted him. Raj is absurdly humble and such an optimist. But the thing that is so overwhelmingly impressive from him is how calm he can be in the middle of a storm. You don't go to Raj to make quick money. And it's never about his bottom line—he's very client-centered. He's more like a family physician, the doctor you start going to at twenty, and you're still seeing at sixty. I see him as a guide to get me from point A to point Z."

- The entrepreneur: "I've always been a conservative investor. I take risks in my business, so I like to play it safe with my portfolio. Raj is really good at putting together a portfolio that meets your goals. He really wants you to use your portfolio to support the life you want to have. And he's always willing to talk to me about my real estate investments or moves I might be making with my business—things that don't make him any money but are important to me and my life. When he's with you, he's with you for your whole economic value set. He really listens. He's always calm and very approachable. And he's wonderfully gracious about sharing his network. I will never forget the day we met my biggest goal of achieving financial independence. I can't tell you how joyous he was when he called me up and told me we'd made it. There was just this human transmission of joy."

- The husband and wife: "Raj is a very patient listener. He always gives you 100 percent of his attention. Even if you ask a 'dumb' question, like what an acronym stands for—the way he answers is the way a good doctor would treat a patient if they asked a question about a treatment. He has a very calm personality. We each have our own pension plans, and Raj has always respected us both and allowed us each to set our own individual risk tolerance. We've been clients for a long time, and our accounts are modest compared to the size of his portfolio, but he's still taking care of us. He's always available to us, which means a lot. Raj is also such a great philanthropist. He believes in causes bigger than himself. He has a global perspective, and he's always involved in trying to uplift people around the world."

I hope you can see some of the themes I've discussed coming through in how my clients talk about me—my long-term holistic approach; my focus on who the client is as an individual and what their goals are; my client-centered, client-first attitude.

Ultimately, your marketing materials can say whatever you want, but your brand really comes from how people perceive you. Your work ethic, your ability to help clients navigate the ups and downs of the market, and the way you treat people will always matter more than any clever slogan you might come up with.

Key Takeaways

- To stand out in a crowded field, financial advisors must specialize and develop their own unique brands.
- That brand can evolve over time; mine has evolved from specializing in doctors to wealth creators.
- Whatever specifics your brand entails, you must include some basic elements that are essential for all advisors.
- Those elements include expertise in all areas of financial planning, investment savvy, an understanding of global economics, a highly qualified team, and a consultative, client-centered approach.
- You must not let your brand go stale; you need to keep up with the times.
- Your longtime clients should be able to speak clearly and well on your behalf.

6

GOAL SETTING

Dream no small dreams for they have no power to move the hearts of men.
—William Goethe

I'm fanatical about setting goals. I set business goals, personal goals, family goals—I believe goals are critical.

Goal setting is important in any field, but it's especially crucial if you're running your own business. When you work for someone else, your boss likely sets most of your goals for you. They dictate what your priorities are and what you need to accomplish by when. But when you work for yourself, that's all up to you. Nobody's going to tell you what to focus on or push you to work harder. You've got to self-motivate and setting goals and working to achieve them can help.

My first month in the business was eye-opening. The office would publish the ranking of the advisors monthly—and I was ranked at the very bottom. Of course, I had no clients yet and was still trying to figure out my overall game plan. But I knew I had to keep up. I couldn't stay stuck at the bottom of that list.

I remember setting a goal of getting to the top fifty after year 1, and then kept moving it up over the years. By year five in the business, I was in the top five in the office. But I kept raising my sights. Over a decade ago, I set a goal of cracking the top five in the entire firm. We accomplished this two years ago.

My basic philosophy on goals is that they should be big. I think it's good to set scary and intimidating goals. Personally, I would get complacent if I stuck with something "realistic." This may not be the right prescription for everyone, but it's certainly worth a try. A too-comfortable goal doesn't motivate me. Even if I fail at meeting a big goal, I will have accomplished something I wouldn't have otherwise. As Brian Tracy, the acclaimed motivational speaker says, "Goals should get you out of your comfort zone."

I also believe in writing goals down. That visualization and written confirmation of what you're aiming for is key. I like to write my goals down on sticky notes and put them up around my office. It's a little hokey, but it reminds me of what I'm supposed to be doing when I sit down at my desk. When my goals are all around me, I'm never far away from knowing what I need to do.

Goal Setting: The Process

I'm sure you've heard of SMART goals—that your goals should be specific, measurable, attainable, relevant, and time-based. That's a great start. I definitely support the idea that you should choose specific goals you can measure so you know if you're on track—goals that are possible but ambitious, goals that are relevant to your big-picture values and objectives, and that you should set deadlines to keep yourself moving. But let's dig deeper.

By this point, I hope it won't surprise you to hear that I believe your goal setting should start with your purpose. Everything flows from your big why, and your goals should be no exception.

I set goals with my team every year. We set one big annual goal, and break that into quarterly team and individual goals. We keep the goals simple—no more than one page. And every time, the first line is our mission statement.

For my team, that means the first line on our goal sheet is about helping our clients achieve *their* goals and dreams. I don't want anybody to forget that. Everything we do should be in service of our mission to support our clients.

Start with your mission. Then choose goals that are related to your mission. Again, I like to keep it simple. With my team, I try to keep it to three *quantitative* goals and three *qualitative* goals. Anything beyond that, and people will forget.

Once you've set your big annual goals, work from that big picture down to the specific. In my office, we do this process as a team—I want everyone to participate. There are fifteen of us, so we'll break into groups of three or four to make sure everyone's voice can be heard. Each group will talk about possible goals, come up with a few suggestions, and then we'll come back together as a team to review and decide.

Once we have our team goals, every person on the team sets individual goals for themselves. Every person on the team has something to contribute to our success, and the goal-setting process helps each member of the team stay focused on what we're trying to accomplish. I also encourage everyone to share their individual goals with the entire team, so we can keep each other accountable.

From those team and individual goals, we then work down to the specific strategies we need to put in place to accomplish those goals. Again, we'll keep it simple—three or four lines per goal—so we can stay focused.

Goal Setting in Practice

Let's look at a couple of examples. A *quantitative* goal for my team might be to gather $200 million in new assets. As a team, we'd talk about how best to accomplish this. We might break that big goal down into smaller goals of signing two new accounts of $50 million each, three accounts of $25 million each, and then make up the rest with $10 million accounts.

From there, every team member would think about what they'd need to do to help the team accomplish that goal. Everyone's role is different, but everyone has a role. For myself and some of my junior advisors, our goals will be things like asking for referrals from existing clients, doing educational events and other outreach, keeping up our thought leadership, and so on—specific things we can do to get our team in front of prospective clients. For someone in a supporting role on our team, their goals might be to ensure that advisors are following up with new contacts within a week, to ensure new contacts are signed up for our newsletter and invited to any webinars or events our team is doing, and so on. All these goals support our big-picture goal of bringing in new assets.

A *qualitative* goal might be something like getting the entire team to embrace a new Salesforce system we've adopted, getting the team to learn to use some new financial planning tools, sharing best practices across the team, or simply continuing our education as a team. It can sometimes be harder to break qualitative goals like these down into specific quarterly actions, so the details are key here. For example, if our team goal is to use the new Salesforce system, then everyone on the team should have individual goals about spending time learning the system, maybe taking a course, then shifting client data into the system by a certain date, and so on.

Qualitative goals can be tricky. One year we set a team goal of mastering our new CRM system. During our mid-year review, I found that we were far from accomplishing this goal. Team members were used to using Outlook for tasks. They were comfortable with their workflow and were skeptical about why they needed to change. In that case, we ended up modifying our CRM goal and making it more modest. It's better to notch up small wins than accomplish nothing at all.

As the team leader, it's also my responsibility to make sure my team has the resources they need to accomplish their goals. So, when I wanted my team to set a goal around continuing education, I first made that goal more specific by suggesting everyone set an individual goal of taking one self-development course during the year. And then I backed that up with resources and made it clear that our team would pay for up to $1,500 in educational costs for each team member, on any topic. Several team members decided to use this benefit to do meditation training, which I wholeheartedly support.

Measuring Progress

Checking in on your progress is a crucial part of the goal-setting process. You should be setting goals that are ambitious enough that you're not going to just meet them all in Q1 and be done with it. You should be setting stretch goals that you may or may not make. Then measure your progress regularly so that you can see that even if you're falling short of your goal, hopefully you're making important progress. For example, if my team set a goal of bringing in $200 million in new assets over the course of a year, and by June we've only brought in $75 million, we're not on track to meet our goal—but we are on track to have a pretty great year. I don't consider falling short of a goal to be a failure. I think falling short is actually an opportunity to reassess your strategy and set it on the right course.

With my team, we check in on our goals as a group once per quarter. The idea for this conversation is to be open and honest with ourselves about what's working and what we might need to do differently in order to meet our goals. Maybe we've discovered that one of our goals was too modest, and we can revise it to be more ambitious. Maybe we're learning that another goal was extremely aggressive, and we probably won't meet it—but we can still talk about what we've learned about ourselves as a team and where that goal is taking us.

I try not to be the messenger on every item. Especially if we're falling behind on a goal, I don't want the team to feel like I'm reprimanding them. I find that's not nearly as effective as an open and honest team conversation about where we're doing well and where we're falling short.

I also check in with each team member individually once a quarter. Everyone has their individual goals that contribute to our team goals and our larger mission, so I like to have a similar conversation about those individual goals. In these conversations, I'll ask questions like, what are you learning from the process of pursuing this goal? What additional resources might you need to accomplish this goal? What do you feel is holding you back from going after this 100 percent? Is there anything the rest of the team can do differently to support you? Do you want to change this goal to make it feel more attainable?

In our regular team meetings, I also encourage people to share success stories every month. These stories may or may not relate to our specific goals for the year, but they should relate to our overarching mission. For us, that means sharing "wow" stories of moments when our team really went above and beyond to help a client. Like the time a client of ours got his wallet stolen in Paris, and we jumped in and took care of everything for him—speaking to his hotel, getting cash and new cards to him within twelve hours. Sharing success stories like these reminds us of all we're trying to do for every client, every day.

Goal Setting When You're Starting Out

Early on, when you're just starting your business, goals are even more important. This is such an entrepreneurial business. There's a direct correlation between effort and success. You can't just cruise along, keeping pace with the people around you. You must set big goals and push yourself to make them happen.

When you work for a big corporation, it's easier to coast. You can hang back and let your boss define your goals. If your department does well, you may get a bonus even if you didn't personally have your best year ever.

But when you work for yourself, it's all on you. You define what you're shooting for, and you control your success.

Early in your career, you should be assessing your progress weekly. You'll want to measure not only your progress toward your goal but your activity in pursuit of that goal. When you're just starting out, you should be shooting for goals that are well out of your immediate reach. You won't get to $5 billion in assets overnight. So you need to know you're doing the work that will get you there.

If you set a goal to network, how many people have you talked to this week? How are you reaching new contacts? Cold calling is obsolete. You need new strategies. Like I did when I was starting out, you need to pick a market segment to target and find ways to connect with people in that segment. Join an association or community group or attend nonprofit events. I used to go to events for the Massachusetts Biotech Society all the time. Most of the content went right over my head, but I still met a lot of clients just by showing up and expressing a genuine interest in their work.

Personal Goals

I take my love of goal setting into every aspect of my life. I set goals for myself both professionally and personally. I write my professional goals on those Post-it notes I mentioned, so I can see them every day as I get down to work. I like to write my personal goals down, too, usually in the first page of whatever notebook I'm using at the moment. Looking back, I'd say my achievement rate is probably 80 or 90 percent—not bad!

My family is probably tired of my goal obsession by now. Since the time my kids were little, I've encouraged them to make New Year's resolutions every year. I probably have the files somewhere, going back for about twenty-five years. Of course, for the past five years or so, my kids have boycotted the process. But even if it hasn't worked for them, it's worked for me. And hey, maybe they'll come back to resolutions in the future. I eventually realized my dad was right, didn't I?

Setting goals that involve other people, of course, is always trickier than setting goals for yourself. One of my goals last year was to teach each of my four kids something about investing. Actually, this has been a goal of mine for the past several years. Because of what I do, it's easy for my kids to just say, "Dad, you take care of it."

I don't need my kids to have the same fascination with the world of investing that I do. But I believe financial literacy is crucial, and it's not taught in schools. So it's important to me that my kids learn at least the basics, like what a balanced portfolio looks like and why a long-term perspective will always win over a focus on short-term gains.

My achievement rate is pretty good. But nobody achieves every single one of their goals. As with business goals, the discipline of setting a goal, writing it down, and working hard to achieve it will take you far in your personal life too. Even if you don't achieve a goal, or don't achieve it right away, if you've applied yourself and worked hard, you will have made important progress.

And if a goal is truly important to you, then when you miss, you just recommit yourself. Like I said, I've set the goal of teaching my kids about investing several years in a row. It's important enough to me that when I haven't accomplished it in a given year, I've recommitted myself and made it a goal for the next year.

Finally, this year, I'm on my way to achieving that particular personal goal—inspiring my kids to learn more about investing. One of the advisors on my team works with my kids, and I've enlisted his help in encouraging them to do some homework before their meetings. In this area, like so many others, persistence and teamwork have paid off.

Another personal goal I've set for myself recently is to set up a scholarship fund for young people who can't afford college. I've informally helped my cousin's kids, and a few other kids in the family, but I wanted to formalize and expand the program beyond my family so I can help young people in the community who have the motivation to go college but cannot afford the hefty cost. It's important to me to give back and help my family, but I don't want it to feel like charity. So I'm working on finding trustees who can administer a more formal process. As a family, we have a charitable foundation that focuses on three areas: education for the underprivileged, disrupting poverty and promoting arts and culture. This has brought our family together; hopefully our kids over time will take on greater responsibility in identifying worthwhile causes and charities.

Nobody lives forever, and the only way people remember you is if you touched their lives in some way. For me, this goal of helping my family achieve their educational dreams is about my legacy—how people will remember me when I'm gone. The same with my goal of teaching my kids about investing. It's all about what I'll leave behind.

Just like your business goals, your personal goals should be connected to your purpose. Don't set goals based on what you think you should want, or what other people expect you to do. Keep your purpose in mind and set your sights on goals that will keep you headed to your true north.

Key Takeaways

- I believe wholeheartedly in goal setting.
- Goals should be clear and actionable, specific, measurable, and attainable.
- I cascade them down from team goals to specific contributor goals to yearly, monthly, weekly, and daily goals.
- You won't achieve all your goals all the time; they need to be flexible.

7

PROSPECTING AND INCUBATING NEW CLIENTS

When you're just starting out, growth is your first, last, and highest priority. You won't survive long if you can't sign clients. But even once you're well established, you'll always have some attrition. Of course, you'll work hard to keep this to a minimum—more on this in below chapters—but some amount of churn is inevitable.

That's why, no matter what stage your business is in, growth should always be a priority. I still want to grow every year. It's simple math, and it's also important motivation for your team. What that focus on growth does is energize your entire team to compete at a high level. It's like high-stake sports. You can't just sit back and do the bare minimum to defend your title. If you don't compete to win, atrophy sets in. The adrenaline of competition is crucial for the long-term survival of the practice. As my good friend and outstanding colleague Dana Locniskar once said, "The only way to coast in this business is by going downhill." To this day, after five decades in the business, Dana is committed to continuous business development.

So how do you find clients? I've already told you that I always avoided cold-calling, even when it was the industry norm. Here are some of the prospecting strategies I've found the most success with.

Being a resource. My goal is always to share the resource of financial planning. I'm not trying to sell; I'm trying to educate. This simple change of perspective is incredibly powerful. You sound completely different to a new contact or prospective client if your goal is simply to share what you know and be helpful.

Of course, your desire to help must be genuine. We've all encountered enough salespeople in our lives. Think about your own experiences: I'm sure you can immediately spot the difference between someone who is genuinely listening out of a desire to help and someone who is just waiting until you're done talking so they can say their thing.

When you're just starting out, it can be tough to maintain this kind of attitude. You need clients. You're always going to be tempted to push and make the deal. Just keep your ultimate goal in mind. You want to start every client relationship the way you intend to go on. As an advisor, you should never be pushing your clients to do anything or selling specific products. You'll be providing information and educating them on financial planning. Start out that way—educate, inform, and begin from a place of trust.

We live in a diverse and dynamic country, with many engines of prosperity. In general, the East Coast of the United States is driven by financial services and health care, the West Coast by technology and social media, the Midwest by manufacturing, parts of the South by energy and resources. Of course, each city or county has its own dynamics. Take the time to really understand the area you live in and try to identify sources of wealth creation. Just look around you to see who the wealthy folks are in your area and how they generated their wealth. This is classic market segmentation analysis, and it's crucial to identifying some target markets.

Every industry segment has an association or networking group, in addition to broader groups, such as chambers of commerce and local colleges and universities. They are always looking for interesting speakers to present to their members. Remember: the operative words are *share your expertise*. Never lead with products—be a resource. Your expertise could be economic and investment strategy, insights on a particular industry, philanthropy, family dynamics, estate tax strategy—the list of potential topics is endless. You just need to be creative in understanding the needs of every segment in your community and share your perspectives.

Concentric circle of referrals. There is nothing more powerful than a referral from an existing client. It gets you 90 percent of the way there. If you're new to the business, referrals may feel like something that just happens. And there's some truth to that—if you're doing a great job for your clients, some referrals will happen organically, simply because your clients are happy with your work.

But you can and should seed referrals deliberately. The Pareto principle, named for an Italian economist, holds that 80 percent of the consequences come from 20 percent of the causes. It applies to a number of fields, and I've always found it's true for referrals—80 percent of my referrals come from 20 percent of my clients.

Start your deliberate referral practice by identifying where 80 percent of your new business came from in the past year. When I did this analysis in 1993, the bulk of our new business came from:

- Anesthesiologists
- Nephrologists
- Neurosurgeons

This past year, 80 percent of our new business came from the following segments:

- Technology entrepreneurs in a post-IPO situation
- Private business owners, particularly in health care, monetizing their equity position
- Wealthy retirees who were looking for a new advisor with a broad, holistic strategy with a particular emphasis on legacy planning and advanced estate strategy. Investment management, in this case, was not the primary driver.

So what do you do with this data? You use this to target your desired segments. Find a way to network with professional associations, provide targeted seminars, and actively seek referrals from existing clients in each of the above segments. You know your service model is resonating with these groups. Go after more clients like your best clients.

Keep in mind that if your client is making money in their industry, they're likely to know other successful people who are also doing well. That's the concentric circle of referrals—one person can introduce you to their entire social world.

Identify your top clients and plant the idea of referrals in their minds. When you meet with these clients, go through your client meeting process as usual: review the status of their account, discuss their objectives, talk about the progress you've made toward those goals, and mention the people on the team who've contributed to that progress.

Then you mention that you're growing your team. Say, "I'd love to get more clients of your investment caliber."

Now you've put the idea in their minds. In my experience, happy clients are eager to help when you put the question to them this way. Often, they'll say something like, "I'm thinking about someone, but I don't know how much money he has."

Your answer: "You aren't likely to know that. That's our job. We'd love to be put in touch."

Of course, even if the client doesn't have a name in mind at that moment, they may follow up later. Whenever the referral comes, it's crucial to say thank you. We often make it a point to send a personalized thank-you note and perhaps a small gift to express our appreciation.

Circles of influence: Clients aren't your only sources of referrals. Other professionals can also be a great help to you. Look for people who sit in the center of circles of influence: CPAs and tax professionals, attorneys who specialize in mergers, estate planners, real estate brokers. Anyone who regularly works with wealthy people can be a great connection and source of referrals.

You can approach these people in much the same way you do your best clients. Deliberately asking for referrals will get you much farther than simply hoping they'll put you in touch with people in their network. But with these kinds of professionals, you should, of course, also be reciprocal. Identify people you'd be happy to recommend to your clients and ask them for referrals. Create a mutually beneficial relationship.

Professional associations: Boston is a major center for the biotech industry. I've always been fascinated by advances in medical technology, so when I learned about a local professional association for the biotech industry, I paid the annual membership fee of twenty-five dollars and joined up. They organized lots of networking events, and I volunteered to help organize events and fundraise. I'm sure most people thought I was a scientist myself.

Looking back, my involvement in this group has led to about fifteen client relationships. Many of the ambitious young scientists I met years ago are successful entrepreneurs today.

Whether it's a professional organization or the local chamber of commerce or the PTA, you've got to be involved in your community. You can't expect clients to just show up at your door—you have to put in the time and be part of the action. The more people you meet, the more potential clients you'll find.

Bandwagon: In the late nineties, I had a client who was a mid-level executive at a start-up company. He was just awarded stock options and restricted stock and wasn't sure how to manage them. I spent a couple of hours with him, talking about the tax implications of these grants, and we developed a five-year strategy for monetization. He was so impressed with the document that he shared it with his CFO and CEO. Today we have over ten clients from this company, with nearly $400 million in fee-based assets.

This is a classic bandwagon strategy: once you have an advocate in a company, you can continue to penetrate the C-suite through referrals. In effect, you become the de facto financial advisor for the entire company.

I have also had success penetrating physician group practices. Remember: you do not lead with a product; you share your expertise freely. You are now a fountain of thought leadership for this group of high-net-worth individuals. What a great way to build your client base without making a single cold call!

Social media: Obviously, I got my start before the age of social media. But it's becoming an increasingly valuable prospecting tool for me and my team. It's a great way to connect with prospective clients. In the past few years, we have received numerous inbound inquiries from LinkedIn. One of them now has more than $50 million with us.

People who've grown up with social media seem to know this instinctively, but everything you post should be in line with the brand you're trying to create. That brand will vary depending on your target market and your personality, but you should always aim to be knowledgeable and professional. Of course, you also need to follow regulatory requirements. Pay careful attention to your firm's policies to ensure your posts are appropriate.

There are a lot of different rules of thumb out there about how to balance posts promoting yourself with posts promoting others' work or sharing information. But the key is that you should be aiming for a balance. You can promote yourself, but you can't only promote yourself. If you strike a healthy balance, people will start to feel like they know you, and they'll be excited to share your successes. When I posted on LinkedIn that I was humbled to be named a Barron's Hall of Fame Advisor, I got 247 likes and 80 comments. I know I wouldn't have gotten that level of engagement if every one of my updates were celebrating myself.

LinkedIn has become a particularly strong source of referrals for us recently. I just signed on a new client who reached out to me on the site. This was a cold email, unprompted by any referral, but because it came through LinkedIn I was able to see that he had professional connections to two of my current clients. I asked them to put in a good word for me, and that really helped make my case. Based on successes like this one, I'm now bringing in a LinkedIn consultant to speak to my team about how we can best use the site within our firm's guidelines.

Don't neglect email either. Whether you have a formal newsletter or a less formal email list, you should be sending out information roughly once a month. Aim for the same tone in your emails as you strike during in-person meetings with prospects: educational, helpful, informative. You're sharing what you know, not selling anything. And remember—a mass update is useful, but a personal email is even better. Your top-priority prospects should be hearing personally from someone on your team at least once a quarter. I've found that thought leadership with a personal note always gets a warm response.

Incubation pipeline: I've always believed in building an incubation pipeline. When I believe someone is going to be successful in the long term, I'm excited to sign them as a client, even if they don't currently meet my minimums. Eighty percent of those clients pay off and become hugely important accounts in the long term—that's a great ratio, well worth investing the time in up-and-coming young people.

Look for ways to deliberately cultivate relationships with young professionals who are on track to success. Since the mid-1990s, my team and I have been working with tech and biotech companies to educate their employees on stock options. That's a great way to connect with young, early career folks who are poised to do great things. When they exercise their options, they need advice, and they end up becoming clients. We've done pre-IPO planning events that have led to great connections. Academic events can also be a great way to meet entrepreneurs.

The kind of relationship you can build with someone when you're advising them *before* they make it big is completely different from the way you connect with someone who's just made millions in an IPO. Once they hit a big payday, lots of advisors will be reaching out to them. They'll be evaluating their options. You'll be competing with every shop in town. But if you help someone out when they're just getting their feet under themselves financially, you create a whole different level of loyalty. You'll become the trusted advisor who's always had their back.

Today our incubation pipeline has over twenty potential clients at any point in time. This is a much-needed investment for your future. We also maintain a database of prospects who we may have talked with over the years. Like I said, every month, we share a thought leadership piece on investment strategy, planning, or a thematic trend. The key is to be thoughtful and selective in what you send. Over the years, many of these prospects have reached out to us to eventually become clients of our team. This requires patience and an eye on the long term. If you are authentic and treat prospects like clients, they will eventually become clients.

You could also consider the children of our current clients part of our incubation pipeline. Many advisors often overlook their clients' kids. With four children of my own, I know I often worry about their financial knowledge and whether they are prepared to assume responsibility for our assets in case of an emergency. So I understand where my clients are coming from when it comes to their concerns for their kids. Achieving a good rate of return is important, but offering to take care of clients' children builds trust and loyalty. You are now the guardian of their legacy.

On our team, we have two designated "next-gen advisors" who help our clients' children with the basics of financial planning and best practices: how to monitor your credit score, contributing to a Roth IRA, maximizing contributions to a 401(k) plan, basic budgeting, and developing an investment strategy.

Take care of these kids—they will be future clients of your team. According to the Institute of Preparing Heirs, 90 percent to 95 percent of offspring leave their parents' advisors upon receiving their inheritance. Clearly, if you do not form a strong bond with the next generation many years in advance, assets will eventually walk out the door. Don't just be their father's advisor. Make sure you are connecting with the eventual beneficiaries of your clients' assets.

Philanthropy: You should never get involved in philanthropic causes *in order to* meet potential clients. Again, people can smell a fake. If you're more interested in handing out your business card than in genuinely being of service to the cause, you'll turn off the very people you're trying to attract.

I am a passionate believer in giving back and enhancing the world around us. I am involved in several local and global causes, and I serve on the board of trustees of my alma mater. Like I said, I never prospect or draw attention to what I do when I am involved with a charity. But I do share my insights and business expertise freely to help these organizations grow and succeed.

Maybe it's simply good karma: you do good and somehow good things happen to you. Over the years, I have been approached by numerous individuals in my charitable circle for advice on personal wealth management—without making a single solicitation!

Becoming active in charitable causes gets you entry into a series of new social circles. I've met some amazing people through my work with foundations. The key when meeting someone famous or influential is not to get tongue-tied. Try to ask them something out of the blue. Think of open-ended questions that will start a conversation. I once met David Lynch, the acclaimed filmmaker, a big proponent of meditation, as I am. I asked him, "Which of your many movies is the most memorable for you?"

His answer was *Dune*, which I happened to have seen the night before.

And remember: Never sell. It's extremely off-putting. Influential people are surrounded by people who want something from them. I never even tell people what I do unless they ask.

Say yes to opportunity: I once went to a charity dinner I knew the CFO of a major financial firm would also be attending. I got there a few minutes early and switched my seat so I could sit next to him. We'd met once before, and I wanted to get to know him better.

We made small talk for a while, and then he asked what I did. I explained, and he asked, "Do you do cash management for corporations?"

I hadn't. But I immediately said, "Of course I do!" I'd been in business long enough by that point to feel confident that, even if I hadn't done cash management myself, I could easily find someone to advise me.

This one conversation landed me a $2 billion cash management account. This was probably one of the largest accounts opened by an advisor in the firm. I took a chance, bet on myself, and said yes to opportunity—and it worked out brilliantly.

Treat everyone with respect: One day, in 1987, a senior broker in the latter stages of his career asked me to handle a walk-in. This broker said, "I can't even understand the guy."

The walk-in was an Asian couple who spoke halting English. I offered them a cup of tea and ended up spending an hour and a half with them talking about their family, life in the United States, and their long-term goals. It turned out they came from an extremely wealthy family back in Asia and had come to the United States to get an education.

If I had dismissed them because they didn't speak English well, I would have missed out on long-term clients whose account is now worth over $100 million, with an additional $50 million in a family foundation. Our team is also the advisor to their four children.

I had a similar experience with a retired schoolteacher I met at a nonprofit event. She asked me to review her retirement account, and as a favor I looked over her investments and talked her through some basic concepts, like asset allocation, risk tolerance, and so on. A few years later, she referred me to her nephew, a successful entrepreneur who's since become one of our biggest clients.

Being kind is always worthwhile. It's good karma to share your expertise with people you meet, regardless of whether they're a "good prospect" or not. In many ways, I believe you become something of a public figure as a financial advisor. It's like being a doctor—if someone asks you about their headaches at a party, you don't tell them to call your office or charge them for your time. You try to help them as best you can. You have an expertise few people have and all people need. Being generous with that expertise is always the right call.

Today I'd say that about a third of my new clients come from networking, a third come from referrals, and a third from social media or thought leadership. No matter where you're meeting people, never prejudge anyone. Approach everyone with an open mind and treat everyone with respect. You never know who you're going to meet next.

Key Takeaways

- You need to prospect continually for new clients, but it should not be a hard sell.
- Think of yourself as a resource for prospective clients.
- Your best source of future clients will be referrals from your existing ones.
- Social media is now a great way to find new clients.
- I have always given back, and while I never solicit clients directly through philanthropic events and causes, they often come to me at those times.
- I keep my incubation pipeline active and full.
- You should treat everyone with respect; you can't always tell a prospective client by the clothes they wear or the way they speak or look.

8

BUILDING AN ALIGNED TEAM

Back when financial advisors were stockbrokers, many people saw this as a hypercompetitive business. I never took this view of my work. Thankfully, the business has caught up with me. Today financial advisory can be a very collaborative business. My team is essential to my success.

Of course, when you're just starting out, you can't exactly afford to hire a great team like mine. But you can still look for ways to collaborate and bring more experience and expertise to your clients.

Let's take a look at building an aligned team in three phases of your career as a financial advisor.

Building a Team as a Newbie

When you're just starting out, you probably can't even afford to hire an assistant. You've got hustle and hunger, but you don't have the experience that many clients will be looking for. High-net-worth clients especially want to feel like they're entrusting their wealth to someone who isn't learning on the job. And yet just one high-net-worth client can really help you establish your book of business when you're in that building phase.

My advice to young advisors trying to land a bigger client is to approach a senior advisor at your firm and ask them to partner with you on the account. Remember: you only get one shot at a prospect. People don't change financial advisors that often. If you miss that big account this time, it probably won't come up for bid again for another ten years, unless something goes seriously wrong to cause dissatisfaction.

Align yourself with someone who has the experience and gravitas to reassure the client that they'll be in good hands. Propose a reasonable split with the senior advisor. The advantage for them is that the account is essentially falling in their lap. You've done the work of identifying the prospect, getting to know them, understanding what their needs are and what might help seal the deal. On your end, of course, you're getting the benefit of the senior advisor's experience, which will likely help you seal the deal.

Working with a senior advisor has other benefits too. They might be able to refer smaller accounts to you. For example, I now have a $10 million account minimum. I make some exceptions, but I'm always looking for smart, dependable, young advisors I can refer business to. If someone's been referred to me, but I can't work with them, I want to make sure they land somewhere they'll be well taken care of. Building your reputation with senior advisors at your firm will do wonders for your business in the long run.

Make sure you pick a senior advisor who's compatible with your potential client. If, for example, you were approaching me, you'd have a higher chance of success if you brought me an up-and-coming wealth creator, an entrepreneur, or corporate executive who would fit well with the rest of my clients. Your goal is to find a senior advisor who handles the type of clients you're bringing in—both for the senior advisor's comfort and for the client's. You'll also learn a lot by observing how your senior partner approaches the account, particularly if this is the type of client they specialize in.

As the junior partner on the account, you'll handle the service and quarterly reviews of the client's portfolio. The senior advisor will provide the investment and financial planning support and service infrastructure.

It can be intimidating to approach a senior advisor. But the business has changed a lot since I started my career. A lot of firms are promoting collaboration more and more. This is the age of teams, not the age of the lone wolf.

As a beginning advisor, you can also create a virtual team who will help you put your best foot forward when potential clients are researching you. A senior partner you're working with, specialists within your firm you can draw on as resources—these can become the members of your virtual team. Investment analysts or financial planners who work for your firm are there to help you serve your clients. Make sure you're using all the resources at your disposal and highlighting that fact. Put these people on your website and talk about how you use these resources with potential clients.

Instead of being an inexperienced solo practitioner, you're an up-and-coming young advisor backed by a great team. I believe advisors don't do this nearly enough. As a young advisor, I didn't know this was even an option. But it's a great way to enhance your brand and dramatically increase your chances of success.

As a new advisor, you must subjugate your ego. Don't try to go it alone. If you reach out and ask for help, your learning curve will be so much shorter. By working with more experienced advisors and specialists, you'll learn a lot about how to approach clients, how to communicate, how to organize a portfolio—a whole range of best practices. The cost of admission is low. You're just putting some names on a website or sharing one or two accounts. As you build your confidence, you can approach bigger and bigger clients on your own. Working with senior people now is an investment in your future.

Even if you don't have an account to share, I'd highly recommend reaching out to a senior advisor and saying something like, "I admire your business and the way you conduct yourself. Can I get a few minutes of your time?"

In my experience, almost nobody says no to a request like this. Very few people make an ask like this because they don't know how to approach the situation. Keep it simple, emphasize that you'll meet at their convenience, and come prepared with thoughtful questions. I made it a practice to sit down with as many senior advisors as I could when I was starting out.

Some younger professionals today are very comfortable with email communication, but less comfortable face-to-face. Ultimately, you're going to have to get comfortable meeting face-to-face. This is a people business. Plus, the senior advisors you'll want to learn from are from an earlier generation, and they'll expect to sit down face-to-face.

When You're Ready to Start Hiring

In most large firms, as your assets under management grow, you'll have the opportunity to hire more people for your team. But if you feel you need to hire more than the firm has approved, you'll need to hire out of your own compensation.

My advice is to stop thinking of this as a job. Obviously, if you worked for IBM, you wouldn't be expected to use your own money to hire more hands for your department. But being a financial advisor isn't a job. It's a business. And businesses succeed when you invest in them.

Ever since I started out, I've reinvested my own money back into my business. I started by reinvesting 5 percent of my income, then 10 percent. Today about 20 percent of my income goes back into the business.

Over the years, I've tended to hire one or two people every couple of years. I look at my current capabilities from a business perspective, identify gaps and weaknesses, and figure out what the team needs most.

My first hire was a client associate. As a young advisor, I was taking on way too many clients. I needed someone who could help me stay organized. The person I hired was so exceptional at organization and budgeting that she eventually became my business manager.

After that, I hired a dedicated financial planner for my team. Then an investment analyst. Today I have five advisors who serve our clients, two analysts, five client associates, a business manager, and a nonpracticing attorney dedicated to helping our clients with estate and tax planning strategy, working closely with outside attorneys and tax professionals.

Your sequence of hires might be different. The key is to think about hiring as the founder of a business. When it's just you, reach out for as much support as you can find. Set aside money to reinvest in your business from day one. It's worth some sacrifice to invest in growing your business.

When you're ready to hire, think strategically. Don't just focus on what would make your life easier. Think about what will allow you to do more for your clients—and take on more clients. That may be an administrative assistant or office manager, or it might be a second advisor or a specialist who can take some work off your plate. Take advantage of opportunities to hire with support from the larger firm, but don't be afraid to take the initiative to hire on your own if you believe it's the right step for your business.

When You're Building Your Team

Your first couple of hires will set the tone for your team going forward. Skill is important, of course, but practical skills can be learned. Here are the top five things I look for when hiring:

1. Ethics. Ethics always must come first. An ethical business is a bulletproof business. In interviews, I always ask people why they're interested in joining the business. If their answer is about making money, that's a red flag. Money is a by-product of doing good for our clients. If you're focused on making a quick buck, that affects your tactics. I'm always looking for people who are motivated by a desire to help others.

2. Shared values. It's important to get to know people during the interview process. I want to hire people who have a sense of

purpose. I want my team to be diverse but have a shared worldview. I also like to hire optimists. The world is sorely lacking a sense of optimism, but this is not a business for pessimists. Markets go up and down, but long-term investors succeed as long as they stick to their plans.

3. Ability to work on a team. Americans tend to value independence, as I learned when I first tried to break into this business. But I don't want people on my team who are so independent that they can't work with anyone else. On my team, I try to cultivate a spirit of compromise and understanding. Everyone should be focused on helping the entire team succeed, together. I had a great analyst a few years back who was very dedicated to her work—so dedicated that she said she didn't want to talk to anyone on the team until 3:00 p.m. That kind of approach just won't work on my team. I won't tolerate toxic behavior from anyone, no matter how good their work is.

4. Willingness to accept responsibility. Everyone on my team must be willing to step up and get the job done. In interviews, I'm always alert to any signs that the person has a tendency to deflect blame or make excuses. I like to hire people who will own up to a mistake, who will volunteer to take on projects, and who are committed to making sure the team meets its goals. I never want to overburden anyone on my team. Work-life balance is very important to me. But I want everyone on my team to have a pitch-in mentality. Of course, along with shared responsibility goes shared rewards—both financial and emotional. I'm always looking for ways to recognize hard work. Things like titles and being singled out for praise in a meeting mean a lot to people.

5. Positive attitude. I always say, "Aptitude can be learned, but attitude can't." I'm not looking for Pollyannas, but a positive attitude, adaptability, and flexibility are critical. The world is changing incredibly fast. You can't be stuck in your ways. I find the most successful people are the ones who always say, "Give me more things to do!" I'm looking for people who are dedicated to learning. I also want people who have that drive to make a mark—I can't have any clock-punchers on my team. Of course, that positive, flexible, results-oriented attitude goes both ways. We've all had to be flexible during COVID. As we started talking about returning to the office, two of my employees reached out and let me know they wanted a more flexible arrangement. One shared that she was saving $500 a month on childcare by working from home and asked if she could continue working from home two days a week. My answer: Of course! I'm always willing to work with someone who has a positive, can-do attitude.

For me, that attitude-over-aptitude concept is crucial to building a successful team. Obviously, you've got to be smart to succeed in this business. The concepts we deal with can be complex, and we must keep track of a lot of details. But ultimately, EQ is as important as IQ, maybe more. Some of the most successful advisors I've worked with have gone to state schools, and some of the least successful have gone to Ivy League schools. Those Ivy Leaguers were supersmart, but they were missing an understanding that they're not the boss—the client is the boss. Nobody wants to hear how smart you are. Clients are focused on what they need, not what's on your agenda.

Working with a Team

Once you've started building out a team, it's crucial to clearly define everyone's roles and responsibilities. But don't get stuck in those roles—regularly reevaluate. As a team leader, your role is to develop the entire team. Every year, I go to everyone on the team and ask them what they're passionate about and what they'd like to do less of. You'd be surprised how often the thing one person doesn't want to do is the thing someone else is passionate about. Look at the team as a whole and look for ways to share responsibilities so everyone can keep growing.

About 50 percent of compensation for my team members is based on the individual's contribution to the team's goals. Again, I don't want Lone Rangers; I want team players. The minute somebody on the team says, "*I* did X," I gently correct them: "*We* won a great account today, and here's why." I'll call out individual contributions along the way but focus on how every success is a team effort.

Today I invest 20 percent of my business income back in my team, every year. Not all of that goes to hiring. A substantial amount goes to team development. I send people to workshops, self-development classes, presentation skills, and so on. When my team succeeds, I succeed, so I'm highly invested in helping my team stretch themselves and grow into the best advisors they can be.

McDonald's has the best french fries in the world. Why? Because they've figured out a repeatable process that produces great fries, every time. All great organizations have clear processes. Once you have a process, you can replicate success again and again. The team I'm building today includes people in their thirties and forties because I want my team to be with my clients not just for their lifetimes but for their kids' lifetimes. When my client's twenty-six-year-old kid is fifty-six, I'll be on a beach in Costa Rica somewhere, but my colleague Brian will still be in the business, working for that family.

My Team Speaks

It's easy for me to talk about how I invest in my team, but the proof is in the relationships I've built. I have much less turnover on my team than most of my peers do, and that's because I'm genuinely invested in my team's success.

Let's hear from a few of my team members.

- *On our brand and core value proposition*: "We've built out this world-class team to deliver peace of mind. Our core expertise is investment management, but it's much deeper than that. Our job is taking care of the individual and their family. We can sit down in front of a potential client and say we've seen your case before—we've dealt with that."

- *On professional development for the team*: "Raj's skill is really identifying people's strengths and giving them the bandwidth to grow and develop within the team. He lets team members determine which direction they want to grow in and lets them grow with the team. People stay for a long time because there are a lot of opportunities to do more, even as a junior member, than you could in other practices."

- *On our working environment*: "There are no slow days with us. There's no one here who hasn't done a conference call on

> a Saturday morning or a Sunday night. That's the ethos of the team—whatever is required is what we'll do. But we also try to find balance and get plenty of time off and family time. Raj sets the tone for our culture—we stay positive, we keep moving forward, and we always do what's best for the client. He's so inclusive, and he makes you feel like you're a part of something."

I'm thrilled that everything I've tried to communicate to my team has come through. That's the real measure of success as a manager—I know I've built an aligned team because my team members all share the same values, focus on the same core principles, and genuinely enjoy working together.

Key Takeaways

- When you are starting out, think about partnering with a senior advisor to get help landing the "big fish" clients.
- As you begin to succeed, you'll want to start assembling a top-notch team.
- For me, that meant a client associate, a financial planner, an analyst, several advisors, a business manager, and an attorney.
- It's important that the team shares ethics, values, team orientation, responsibility, and a positive attitude.
- I invest 20 percent of our profits back into the team every year.

9

CREATING A CLIENT BILL OF RIGHTS

I've learned that people will forget what you said, people will forget what you did, but people will never forget how you made them feel.
—attributed to Maya Angelou

We've talked about some strategies for finding clients. Of course, signing clients is only the first step. You've got to maintain strong relationships with those clients over many years.

The basics of client relationship management are simple. First and foremost, as an advisor, you must always act in your client's best interest. You must behave ethically. You must understand your clients' needs, create appropriate plans that will help them meet their goals, and communicate regularly with them to ensure they understand what you're doing and why. Almost any financial planner would say that those are their intentions. The way you differentiate yourself and keep your clients happy for the long term is in how you execute on those big-picture goals.

In order to consistently execute for your clients, you've got to establish clear processes. You can't just react to client requests—you'll get buried in questions, and you'll fall behind on executing your plans. Process ensures that nothing falls through the cracks.

Process is also what makes success repeatable. You might be able to muddle through without a clear process when you're just starting out, and you only have a handful of clients. But as your business starts to grow, you'll find that you simply have too much to do to keep working on an ad hoc basis. And once you start hiring people to join your team, having clear processes is crucial to ensuring that your clients are well taken care of no matter who is executing a particular task. As your team grows, you want to ensure that your entire team provides the same consistent level of service.

One way to start establishing those repeatable processes for success is to create a Client Bill of Rights. Set out about ten things that every client can expect from you—things that you intend to build your brand around—and then work from those broad principles down to the detail of the processes you'll need to hit those big goals.

Reevaluate your processes at least once a year. Are you succeeding? Is anything falling through the cracks? Are there any places to streamline and make things more efficient? Any new tools that could help you do your job better? There are lots of software options out there now that are designed to help you manage customer relationships.

Let's take a look at my team's Client Bill of Rights. I'll share the broad principles, and then we'll look at each one in a little more detail and talk about how we execute on these principles in practice.

Our Client Bill of Rights

Every client deserves:

- An investment policy summary and a financial plan.
- Systematic and predictable contact, reviews, and meetings.
- A proactive, not reactive, approach to asset management, planning, and service.
- A transparent and fair pricing model.
- Regular communication, education, and dissemination of information.
- Prompt attention to requests and phone calls on the same business day.
- Notification of progress and time line.
- For us to listen, listen, and listen more. Our goal is to understand, empathize, and create concrete action plans in collaboration with our clients to accomplish their goals and objectives.
- A personalized, high-touch approach to service.

My team and I share this Bill of Rights with new clients. We want to set the tone and let them know what they can expect from us.

We also want them to hold us to these high standards. In some businesses, it may make sense to underpromise and overdeliver. But I believe that when people are entrusting you with their money and their goals for the future, you need to show them from the beginning that you take that responsibility very seriously. You want to impress your new clients by showing them how hard you intend to work on their behalf, and then you've got to execute to that high level.

Let's look at each of these principles in a little more detail to see how each principle suggests some processes for long-term success.

An investment policy summary and a financial plan. Every client is different. They have different risk tolerances, different goals, and different needs. As a financial advisor, you will have your own investment style, including your take on where the market stands, asset classes you favor, and so on. But every client needs and deserves their own customized investment policy statement that reflects their individual risk tolerance and their own financial plan that lays out how you intend to help them achieve their goals.

In terms of process, we develop a plan for each client when we begin a new relationship. We check in on the plan every quarter. We ask every quarter if anything has changed in terms of the client's current financial situation or their long-term goals, and we revise the plan as needed. If we meet a goal, we celebrate—and then we talk about what's next and make a new plan.

Systematic and predictable contact, reviews, and meetings. Predictability creates a lot of comfort for clients. It also helps streamline our processes. Predictable portfolio reviews and check-in meetings won't eliminate other calls or questions that come up in between meetings, but they can reduce the number of client calls we end up fielding. We set out the cadence of meetings with clients when we begin a relationship, we send out reminders in advance of every check-in, and we always mention the next meeting on the schedule before closing out any call.

A proactive, not reactive, approach to asset management, planning, and service. Clients should never feel like they have to hunt us down. In the absence of a crisis or change in circumstance, we should be reaching out to clients more often than they are reaching out to us. We're also proactive when it comes to asset management. We make a plan and put money to work on a schedule, never in reaction to market moves.

Process-wise, this principle comes down to client communication and client education. We do a basic education webinar or meeting with every new client in which we talk about our philosophy of asset management and our approach to investing. Going forward, we do regular educational events for all our existing clients to share our thoughts on the markets and economic trends.

A transparent and fair pricing model. This one should be obvious. I believe in being radically transparent with clients. Any sources of compensation beyond client fees should be disclosed up front, without the client having to ask, and your billing policy should be fair and consistent for all clients. In his debut book, *Transparency Wave*, my dear friend and fellow advisor Paul Pagnato talks about the six Ts of exponential transparency: transparency standards, terms, total accountability, transparent cost, trust, and trust. These six foundational principles have the potential to transform any business, particularly wealth management.

Regular communication, education, and dissemination of information. Of course, we must keep our clients updated about our progress toward their goals, and any changes in their accounts. But we also aim to provide regular thought leadership. We organize educational events for clients on a quarterly basis. These days, these are typically webinars. We also send out thought leadership updates to all clients at least once a month, and we strive to reach out personally to clients with educational materials targeted to their interests. Recently, we sent out a thought leadership piece on family discussions around wealth. Many clients forwarded the piece to their friends. One of them reached out to us and is in the process of starting a $20 million-plus relationship with our team!

I believe it's part of our job as financial advisors to help our clients learn to be better investors. That means sharing our perspective as well as updates on big-picture economic trends and international news that could affect our clients' investments. Our clients find a lot of value in this kind of education.

Prompt attention to requests and phone calls on the same business day. This is primarily a staffing issue. When I was just starting out, I got to a point where I had taken on so many clients that I couldn't return calls on the same business day. Being a financial advisor is a high-trust position. You are literally handling people's futures. You must be able to get back to people quickly in order to maintain that trust. If you are finding that your team is having trouble answering messages and responding to questions, it's time to hire more staff.

Notification of progress and time line. Again, this is about transparency—and education. Clients should get in-depth updates on their progress every quarter. These should be live meetings, either in person or over a secure video call. Each of these meetings should revisit the time line you've established for meeting specific goals. Are you making the progress you expected? Does the time line need to be adjusted? It's important to educate clients about realistic expectations. If someone comes in expecting a 20 percent annual return with zero downside risk, it's your job to show them why that's not a reasonable expectation and explain what kinds of returns they can expect from different asset classes.

For us to listen, understand, and empathize with their goals and objectives. Empathetic listening is an essential part of the service we provide to clients. Money is a sensitive topic in our society, and you need to show clients they can trust you with a true picture of their financial position and an honest account of what they want their lives to look like. Providing this level of service starts with client selection. This is another reason not to just target any rich person—if you are silently judging a client for their goals or their lifestyle, they will sense it, and you won't be their advisor for long. I like to target wealth creators—entrepreneurs or corporate executives—in part because I feel like I understand and can relate to them. I also know first-generation wealth creators have a learning curve when it comes to adjusting to their new financial circumstances, and I can help. Targeting clients you can relate to in some way can help you start off on the right foot as you are building your practice. From there, it's up to you and your people skills.

Also, never underestimate your client's intelligence or ignore their input. After all, you are handling their hard-earned savings, and it is crucial to understand their preconceived notions or expectations. Our job as advisors is to simplify complex ideas so clients can relate to them. I implore my colleagues not to use industry terms, such as alpha, beta, standard deviation, and the like. It may sound impressive to you, but for most clients it's intimidating and will prevent them from working with you.

A personalized, high-touch approach to service. Back-end systems can help you and your team achieve the high-touch service all clients deserve—and high-net-worth clients expect. Make sure you're taking notes during each meeting with a client. If you have an assistant or junior advisor on your team, you can have this person take notes so you can give your full attention to the client. Collect these notes in a centralized database so that anyone on your team who touches the client has access to the most up-to-date information about their goals, their lifestyle, and any other information that might be relevant.

As the primary advisor on a client account, you need to be prepared prior to a review call or meeting. I spend at least a half hour with our team reviewing our CRM notes, past rebalancing, and overall progress. Also, make sure you remember personal details: names of children, birthdays, milestone events, family, and other goals. Believe me: More than investment performance or asset allocation, your empathy and personal connection with your client will make all the difference in the world. Nothing will replace empathy and personal connection.

These days, because I am conscious of succession planning with my team, I want my junior partners backing me up on any account to have these kinds of details at their fingertips too. But as you're building your practice, succession planning is less of a concern. The key is to ensure that clients don't have to repeat themselves. If a member of your team is interacting with a client, they should know the client's major goals, the status of their accounts, and what was discussed at the client's last meeting with the team. You can be the primary point of connection for the personal relationship, but the rest of your team should also be forming their own relationships with the client, and they should never ask the client to remind them what they've already discussed or what their goals are.

Personalization is also about listening—not just to the details of the client's life but to their goals and philosophy. Every person is different. I have one client who works for herself who prefers to take very little risk with her investments because she knows her income is never guaranteed. I have other clients who are entrepreneurs who like to invest in start-ups—an inherently high-risk endeavor—because they feel their business expertise helps them spot winners. Some high-net-worth clients want to ensure their kids will always be comfortable; others want their kids to work so they learn the value of money. Some people dream of retiring early; others would hate to get out of the game.

Never assume that you know what a client is going to want. Listen to what they have to say, develop an understanding of who they are, and then develop personalized plans from there. Financial planning is not a one-size-fits-all business.

You should also be willing to customize your communication style to suit the client. Some people are in their email inboxes all day; others prefer the phone. Some like to call the office to schedule a meeting; others love a service in which they can schedule a call online. Offer as many options as possible to your clients and learn their preferences.

No Ask Too Small

The final principle in our Client Bill of Rights gets at something that's central to the way I operate my business. For me, nothing ethical is off-limits with my clients. I am happy to offer estate planning services to clients, even though it's technically a "loss leader," because I believe in providing holistic financial planning, and estate planning is a crucial part of a family's overall financial health. I'm also happy to answer business questions, connect clients to lawyers or tax professionals or potential mentors—I'll do anything to help a client succeed. Ultimately, their success is my success. Working my network is a clear value-add that I can offer to clients.

Many of our ultra-high-net-worth clients might have more than one advisor. That's not unusual; most clients like a diversity of approaches. If you want to get a greater share of your client's assets, however, you need to understand their pain points and their situation holistically. We offer our clients a consolidated report every month tracking their asset allocation, performance, tax summary, risk parameters, and several other metrics across various firms. Over the years, we have been able to capture the lion's share of our clients' assets because we position our team as the "coordinating advisor" or as "first among equals."

In 2007 we started a new relationship with an entrepreneur for $10 million. This sum represented less than 10 percent of his assets, which were spread across six firms. Over the past decade, we offered several value-added services to simplify our client's life: a consolidated tracking report across firms, estate planning strategy, discussion on family dynamics, engaging with his children, regular conversations with the family's external tax and legal advisors, as well as sharing philanthropic ideas and strategies. As a result of our intentional approach to adding value, we now have more than 80 percent of this family's total assets. The entire family account is now over $100 million!

One more unwritten rule: do not say anything to impugn the motives or strategy of another advisor or firm. This will surely backfire on you. Sharing your overall insights in a respectful manner is absolutely appropriate, but always be diplomatic.

Recently, my team has even started connecting some of our clients to concierge services offered by Merrill Lynch's Family Office group. Basically, the richer clients become, the more complicated their lives become. Many of our clients are at a point in their lives when they have multiple properties, they travel often, and they're still busy running a business. Concierge services take care of the details, like ensuring sure bills are paid on time, organizing dog walkers, tracking outside investments, obtaining health care in a foreign country, or making sure that the fridge is stocked when they show up at their beach house. This kind of service used to be reserved for the superrich, but increasingly it's available to more ordinary high-net-worth individuals. And who wouldn't like to show up at a vacation home that's already fully stocked?

If a client asks me, "Do you do *X*?" I'll say, "Our team doesn't do that, but let me think about who does and look into it." These kinds of calls prove that clients trust me. I'm the first person they think of when they have any kind of question involving money. That means I'm doing my job! The ultimate objective is peace of mind for the client so they can focus on what they enjoy.

Key Takeaways

- In order to succeed with your clients, you need to behave ethically, understand their needs, create a plan to meet those needs, and communicate regularly.
- Those are the basics. In order to keep succeeding at a high level, you need repeatable processes.
- In order to keep those processes focused on the right things, my team and I have developed a Client Bill of Rights.

- The Bill of Rights helps the team know how best to serve the clients.
- No request is too small, as long as it is reasonable. I often give business advice when I can, or find the right person to help.
- Now that my team and I are servicing ultra-high-net-worth clients, I provide concierge services for these busy, successful people.

10

RUNNING A GREAT MUTUAL DISCOVERY MEETING

When you talk, you are only repeating what you already know. But if you listen, you may learn something new.
—Dalai Lama

Every potential client relationship starts with a single conversation. I like to call this first meeting a mutual discovery session. I always use this exact phrase with potential clients because I want to emphasize the fact we're both exploring whether this relationship will be a good fit. They're learning about me as an advisor, and I'm learning about them as potential clients. They may or may not end up wanting to work with me; I may or may not end up wanting to work with them.

Running a meeting like this is an art form. I've been honing my skills for years. And I'm about to give you a glimpse into my process.

Open-Ended Questions

I believe Terry Gross of National Public Radio is the one of the most intuitive interviewers in broadcasting. Her conversations focus only on the subject. You can tell she prepares extensively for every interview, and she asks thoughtful, open-ended questions that take the conversation in interesting directions. She listens intently and is completely focused on the person she's talking to.

Listen to some Terry Gross interviews and learn from her technique. Remember to always ask open-ended questions that prompt your prospective client to talk—avoid yes-or-no questions. They won't advance the conversation.

Being a financial advisor is a little like being a therapist. You need this person to open up and share about something that is typically considered taboo to talk about: money. I look at this first meeting as an opportunity for me to understand the person in front of me. I want to know about their biggest dreams, their aspirations, and any concerns or reservations they might have about working with an advisor.

I never discuss markets or investments in this first meeting. The first meeting is all about getting to know the potential client. The second meeting is where I'll present my initial thoughts on how we might put their money to work and present broad ideas on estate and legacy planning strategies. After that, we'll make our decisions about whether we're going to work together. And yes, I do turn down potential clients, and you should too.

Let's walk through how I typically start off these mutual discovery sessions, question by question, starting with the big picture.

"Please tell me your story—your life journey." I always start with some version of this simple question. Pause after asking and wait for them to begin talking.

Most people have never been asked for their life story. It makes them feel important and valued. You'll be surprised at how much you can learn with this one simple prompt. I met with a potential client recently, a couple, and this one question got them talking about their lives, how they met, how she put him through school, and more. They spoke for almost thirty minutes without me asking a single follow-up question. They even told me about some health challenges they'd faced and how they struggled to start a family. Then a follow-up question got them talking about their kids for another five minutes.

Listen carefully and ask follow-up questions. Entrepreneurs are often particularly eager to share their stories of success and failure. A client's response to a broad, open-ended question like this will tell you a lot about their philosophy, their approach to life, and the way they function.

I never interrupt potential clients during conversations like these. In another recent mutual discovery meeting, I had to surreptitiously text my partner to remind him to let this potential client finish his story. The rudest possible thing to do in a meeting like this is to say you have to wrap up the meeting. This is the first impression you're making on your potential client—you want to demonstrate to them that they will always be your top priority. I always give meetings like these at least an hour and a half to ensure we can take our time and not feel rushed.

"Could you please describe your goals—the key things you'd like to accomplish in your life?" Again, leaving this question broad and open-ended allows the potential client to reveal a lot about how they think simply in what comes to mind first. Some possible responses include retirement, financial independence, philanthropy, or a lifestyle goal, like buying a vacation home.

Take careful notes, writing down the client's exact responses. I often refer back to these answers in future conversations with clients. This is a great way to show you've been listening, and you care about helping them achieve their goals. Ultimately, your potential client's goals are your job description—this will be what you're working to achieve. So it's crucial that you understand what they really want and that you feel enthusiastic about working to achieve those goals.

Many people want to achieve the elusive goal of "financial independence." I tend not to use the word "retirement" much anymore, as it has negative connotations. Today most people are focused on their life journey and want to contribute in some fashion for as long as possible. They may choose to cut back on full-time employment and devote more time to their family or charity but still stay involved with their careers. In other words, they want to take back time so they can focus on things that are important to them. They want to be strategic, not tactical.

"What is the purpose of your wealth?" This is one of the most powerful questions you could ask. Many people haven't thought about this question this way. But as they think aloud about their answer, you'll learn a lot about their personality and motivation. Over the long term, as I work with clients, I like to try to nudge them to think about their legacies and about how they might want to give back. Prompting clients to think about the purpose of their wealth is a way to subtly start introducing this theme into the ongoing conversation we're having.

"Do you have children? Can you tell me about them?" I try to develop a family tree for every client. This is a simple way for everyone on the team to understand our clients and their goals. Knowing if a client is saving for college or thinking ahead to the kind of legacy they will leave their children helps us fill out the picture of who they are and get a better sense of what we need to deliver for them. And people love talking about their kids!

"Are there people in your family you need to take care of, either now or in the future?" This is a great question for opening up a conversation about aging parents, but, of course, you might also learn about a sibling who needs support, the client's commitment to helping the children of family members, or another issue that will help you understand their needs.

Getting into the Details

Once you get an idea of the big picture—the client's overall vision and goals for their life, their personality, what motivates them, and so on—it's time to pivot to financials. I always start this portion of the conversation by reassuring the potential client they can speak freely: "Our meeting today is totally confidential, regardless of whether we work together or not. This is a bond of confidentiality that is sacred to us."

Then I'll start getting into the details that will help me understand where the client's assets are right now and what kinds of moves I would need to make if I became their advisor. Let's walk through a few of these detail-oriented questions in turn.

"Please tell me about your balance sheet." This is a good, overarching question to start the conversation. It should help you get a snapshot of where their assets and liabilities stand today. Your goal is to understand their current investments, any real estate holdings, business interests, and so on.

"Are you the beneficiary of any trusts?" or, "Are you expecting an inheritance?" These questions help me start to understand a couple of key ways the client's financial situation might change in the future. If they're a beneficiary of a trust, I want to know the status of the trust: Are they currently drawing money from it? How large is the trust, and do they expect it to be exhausted at some point in the future? If they haven't started drawing from the trust yet, what conditions do they have to fulfill to begin drawing down the trust? And, of course, if they're expecting an inheritance in the future, that can help us understand how much they need to save for their needs twenty or thirty years down the line.

These questions can also clue you in to whether there may be additional wealth in the family. If your potential client has wealthy parents, grandparents, or other relatives, that can be a great way to continue expanding your business. Of course, you never want to push. Focus on doing a great job for the client in front of you, and if you prove yourself, and they become comfortable with you, they might eventually recommend you speak to some of their relatives.

"Tell us about your estate planning." You'd be amazed how many people have made a plan in their minds but haven't followed up on the details. Maybe they intend to establish a trust for their children, but they haven't funded the trust. These are crucial details to follow up on.

This is also a great opportunity for me to share my team's value proposition. If their estate plan is incomplete, I'll share with them that this is a very common situation, but that unfortunately it can lead to paying a lot in taxes. I'll explain that my team has an estate planning strategist who takes care of these things. Not all financial advisors offer this kind of service, so now I've had the opportunity to highlight something unique that my team offers.

I would recommend asking clients about estate planning

whether or not you can offer this service in-house. But you can also use this technique to highlight some other differentiating service you're able to provide. If your prospective client is wealthy, you're almost certainly not the only advisor they're meeting. Your primary goal in this meeting is to show them the sensitive, empathetic service you intend to provide. But if you can also find ways to call out some of the practical things that set your team apart, even better!

"Do you have adequate insurance coverage?" This is another area of vulnerability for many new clients. I like to ask specifically about life insurance and umbrella liability coverage. Umbrella liability coverage is crucial for clients who own rental properties. If someone injures themselves on that property, they could sue your client for millions. But if the client places the property in an LLC and gets umbrella liability coverage, their personal assets are protected for an extremely reasonable fee.

"Do you have a net worth statement?" Some people do, but many don't. If a potential client says no, I mention that developing and maintaining a net worth statement is a service we provide to all our clients. Again, the process of profiling a new client is also an opportunity to emphasize your team's best practices.

"How often do your advisors—estate, tax, legal—communicate with each other?" I find that in most instances no one is coordinating external advisors. So this becomes another opening to add our team's value proposition. I might say, "One of the things we do for our clients is communicate actively with their tax and estate advisors so we are all on the same page, working to accomplish our clients' goals."

"I understand you have had advisors in the past. Please tell me what worked in those relationships and what was missing." Understanding past experiences with advisors is important. Of course, you want to be respectful of their past relationships. But it's important to know what they liked and disliked about how their previous advisor worked. Often, folks will say something like their advisor did well for them but didn't address their estate planning issues. Or they'll share that their advisor didn't actively communicate with them. The client's response to this question will give you some clues as to what you need to focus on to win their business.

"If you were to imagine an ideal relationship with an advisor, what would that look like?" Understanding expectations is also key to success in a client relationship. This kind of question can provide clues about their expectations regarding portfolio returns, communication, transparency, and other issues.

If a client says something like, "I want to beat the S and P by five percent," or, "Make me twenty percent a year, and I'm good," it's important to push back. You can't begin a relationship based on unrealistic expectations. This is a legal risk as well as an ethical problem and a recipe for an unhappy relationship.

The Second Meeting

After the mutual discovery meeting, the second meeting is the formal proposal. This is like an audition. You need to get prepared for this proposal meeting like an athlete preparing for a competitive event. In fact, for almost every second meeting, my team organizes a dress rehearsal to ensure we are all in unison on our pitch, the order in which we'll present each element, cues that will let team members know when to jump in and speak, and how to handle unanticipated questions or surprises. Going through this exercise has dramatically improved our closing ratio, which is now between 80 and 90 percent.

I'd estimate that winning a prospective client's business is about one-third dependent on the financial plan you put together, one-third on your team and the services you offer, and one-third simply on the personality match.

As an advisor, your "bedside manner" is very important to winning new business. I don't have to like my landscaper. He could have a terrible personality. But as long as he does the work, we don't need to have much of a personal relationship. But financial advisory is a personal service business. People have to like you. They have to feel you are honest, authentic, and competent, but also humble. Humility is a very powerful value.

Here's a brief overview of how I run a proposal meeting:

We start off the meeting with a summary of our prospect's goals and objectives. In fact, as much as possible, you want to use the exact words your prospect used to describe their goals in your first meeting. This is where you prove you were listening, and you understood what they told you about their goals and philosophy. When you've finished, ask if the summary was accurate. At each stage of the proposal, you want to leave time to pause, clarify, and check your assumptions. That way you can course-correct if necessary.

Next is the wealth planning process. Here you are presenting a comprehensive financial plan—a document that reflects their ideal lifestyle expenses, expected date of retirement or financial independence, cash flows from various sources, potential taxes, and a scenario analysis based on a variety of return assumptions.

It is always best to be conservative in estimating expected rates of return. Plan for the worst-case scenario, but implement strategies to achieve the best outcome. Once you've presented the plan, it's time again to pause and ask the crucial questions: "Are we on the right track? Does this plan make sense?"

The next step is presenting your overall investment strategy with specific recommendations customized for the prospect's objectives. Here we include a few stress tests to demonstrate how the portfolio may fare in a market downturn or a rise in interest rates.

Next we talk about what they can expect. We review our Client Bill of Rights and our communication process. We also include a schematic of their team within our group—the relationship managers, analysts, and client service officers they'll come into contact with.

Be radically transparent in presenting the fee and display every detail possible. This will enhance your chances of closing the sale. Clients only worry about fees if they aren't sure they're getting a great value. We almost never get any push back on our fees, because we have emphasized our service model and process in detail.

Finally, our closing comment is, "If you'd like to speak to a few of our clients, we will be happy to arrange a call or meeting." Making this offer proactively reflects your team's confidence and track record. Make sure you periodically ask your best clients if they're willing to talk to potential clients so you always have a couple of names you can share. If you're doing your job right, your satisfied clients will be your best closers.

Key Takeaways

- Every client relationship starts with a single conversation.
- I recommend asking open-ended questions, such as "What has your life journey been?"

- I also ask about goals, purpose, children, and the details of the client's wealth.

- Then, at the second meeting, my team and I present the proposal.

- Preparation for this meeting is crucial.

- In the second meeting, I offer a summary of the first meeting, a detailed financial plan, the strategies involved in realizing the plan, the expectations of all concerned, and an opportunity to talk to current clients.

11

CONTINUOUS EDUCATION

Commit yourself to lifelong learning. The most valuable asset you'll ever have is your mind and what you put into it.
—Albert Einstein

I met with a prospective client recently who had just sold a company to a private equity firm. After the mutual discovery meeting, we put together a possible financial plan for him, projecting what his lifestyle could look like if he retired in a few years, as he'd shared that he hoped to do. We determined that, given his assets, a conservative estimate of their growth over time, and his lifestyle needs, by age one hundred he would have a surplus of over $15 million. So we suggested that he take some money now and put it into an irrevocable dynasty trust for his kids. This way, it is still family wealth, but the growth is outside his estate, thereby reducing the overall estate tax burden.

His response was literally, "So how do I transfer money to you?"

If I didn't know a few things about estate planning, I never would have won that account. And in fact, when I started out as an advisor, I *didn't* know much about estate planning. But I've continued to educate myself about new developments in the field throughout my career.

My focus on continuous education has won me many accounts. I think it's crucial to my success. But it's easy to say, "Education is critical." Let's take a closer look at how I approach lifelong education.

Personal Education

Let's say you need brain surgery. You go to consult with a surgeon, whose office is full of books. You ask him a question, and he dusts off one of the books and looks up the answer. That doesn't inspire any confidence!

As a financial advisor, people expect you to be knowledgeable. Sure, for very technical questions you can always give a general answer and then back it up with research. But clients want to feel like you know what's happening in the markets, what types of assets are a good buy or not a good buy right now, and so on. They want to feel like you have that information at your fingertips without doing a lot of research.

Investment trends are constantly changing, the markets are constantly changing, and you want to be up-to-date. We all have access to so much information—all you need to do is invest the time.

Set up a system for yourself—block out time in your schedule so you can ensure you have time to read. I like to set aside time in the morning to read and think. I find it's useful to separate thinking time from action time. Once you begin moving through the day's to-do list, you're mentally in the wrong space for deep thinking.

I typically get up at 5:30 a.m. My first act of the day is to meditate for thirty minutes, a practice I have been following for over forty years. Then I will read research and strategy reports for an hour, then tune in to my company's internal "squawk box" for an update on stocks and investment strategy from our worldwide network of analysts. After that, I have more thinking time before I begin making client calls at 10:00 a.m.

I subscribe to five newspapers at home: the *Wall Street Journal, Barron's*, the *New York Times*, the *Boston Globe*, and the *Financial Times*. I also regularly read the *Economist, Businessweek*, and *Forbes*. I always get something valuable out of my reading time. And, of course, I read books. I'd recommend setting aside a minimum of two to three hours a week for reading about the global economy, macrotrends, and thought leadership.

Your goal is not just to broaden your mind but to stay up-to-date on political and economic trends. Clients will look to you to explain things to them—they'll ask you about the housing market, the latest trends in tech, the impact of AI, and a million other questions. You need to be broadly knowledgeable as well as a deep expert in your field.

Professional Education

As much as you need to stay up-to-date on political and economic trends, you also must stay up-to-date on trends in wealth management. Again, if I weren't current on estate planning, I wouldn't have landed that account I mentioned at the beginning of this chapter. More broadly, keeping up with the latest trends in the field is just part of being a professional. If you asked your doctor about a new medical study you'd read about in the news, and she had never heard of it, you'd lose confidence. You want professionals you work with to know what's new in their field and, if they aren't practicing the latest techniques, to have a strong reason as to why not.

You don't have to do this all by yourself. Of course, you should take initiative and go to seminars, conferences, and take opportunities to learn about new trends and techniques wherever you can. But you can and should rely on your firm, your team, and your colleagues to help you stay current.

I'm a data junkie. Merrill Lynch produces hundreds of reports a day, all of them packed with information and new recommendations on asset management. Any large firm will have analysts and other thought leaders on staff—take advantage of those resources.

My team and I also work together to help each other stay up-to-date. Every week we have a thirty-minute learning session, where someone from the team shares a new technique or tool that we can all use. For example, one of my team members recently shared about a client tool called My Financial Picture. It's a free tool within the Merrill Lynch website that automatically creates a kind of balance sheet by constantly updating information from all the client's assets and investments. Only about 10 percent of clients use it because client associates haven't been talking about it. Now that the team has been fully briefed, we can advise more clients to use this convenient free tool.

We make sure to rotate these teach-and-learn sessions through the entire team so we all benefit from as many points of view and areas of expertise as possible. We're stronger as a team than any of us could be alone.

If you are just starting out and don't have a team to draw on, or if you have set up shop as an independent advisor and can't draw on the resources of a large firm, you can still reach out to colleagues to share knowledge. Share information and best practices that you come across and cultivate connections who will do the same for you.

Networking

I've been doing that kind of networking since I started out as an advisor. I now have my own informal "board of advisors" I like to consult about investment strategy. These are people in the business I've gotten to know over the years. Some are retired, some work at other companies, and some are colleagues.

If you work for a large firm, you'll have access to your firm's investment analysis. It's important to keep up with your firm's current recommendations on strategy. But keep an open mind and connect with as many knowledgeable pros as you can.

Active, purposeful networking can help you build this kind of network for yourself. I know networking can feel uncomfortable for some people. But if you're going to succeed as a financial advisor, you'll need to learn to network effectively. Try to focus on building genuine relationships. My "board of advisors" is made up of people whose opinions I respect, of course, but these people are also friends and colleagues I care about.

It takes effort to build relationships like these and to maintain them over the long term. With professional contacts like these, I'll send them a gift every year for the holidays—maybe a bottle of wine or a gift basket—and I'll keep in touch by reaching out to them about once a quarter.

It's taken time and attention, but today I could pick up the phone and call one of the foremost prognosticators of interest rates in the world. I've found his perspective incredibly helpful over the years. Start building your "board of advisors" today, and in a year or two you should have at least two or three people you can call for perspective on investment strategy or market events.

Remember: professional relationships like these should always be a two-way street. Share what you're learning about investment strategy. Share best practices you've discovered. Share contacts who could be helpful. Aim to give as much value to the relationship as you're getting from it.

Best Practices

Sharing best practices can be enormously educational. As part of my focus on continuous education within my team, I encourage everyone to share what they're learning on the job.

When something goes wrong, we'll hold a postmortem as a team to talk about what went wrong and what we can learn from the experience. Everyone makes mistakes; the purpose of these meetings is not to accuse anyone of anything or blame anyone for a lost account or other issue. But it's important to learn from your mistakes and figure out how to do better next time. A postmortem meeting is aimed at openly and honestly talking about what we did well and what we could have improved. Then we'll plan to improve any processes that let us down.

Part of leading a team means having tough conversations when things don't go well. My goal is always to put the focus on what we can learn and how we can improve. When I need to have a performance conversation like this, I'll try to start with the positive:

"Ninety percent of what you're doing is working great, but there are three things I really need you to work on improving." I never want my teammates to get discouraged. Everyone makes mistakes, and everyone has room to improve.

I also believe in sharing success stories. Most teams don't take enough time to celebrate their wins. And it's just as important to learn from your wins as from your failures. When we land a big account, for example, we'll get together as a team to celebrate the win and talk about what went right. Each person on the team will share how they contributed to winning that new client's business. This is a great way to learn best practices from one another.

Going over your wins can also help you turn single successes into repeatable processes. For example, take the new client I mentioned at the beginning of this chapter. If we didn't typically talk about estate planning with potential clients, reviewing this win might lead us to decide to add estate planning to our list of topics to review with all potentials.

Professional Development

Continuous education is not just something I believe in for myself. I believe in education for my entire team. That's why I devote resources to providing everyone on my team with professional development every year.

There are many different forms of professional development. Members of my team have taken classes on public speaking, Excel, meditation, how to present proposals effectively, and more. This is a way for me to reinvest in my business and ensure it continues to grow.

If you're on your own, it's even more important for you to devote time and resources to professional development. This is a way for you to invest in yourself and your future success. You should set aside time and money every year to develop your skills.

Think strategically about what you and your team need. If you're not closing as many new clients as you'd like, you might think about developing your presentation or public speaking skills or brushing up on some of the latest trends in investing and asset management. If you're struggling to keep up with client communication, there's probably a software tool you could learn to use that could help you streamline your processes. And if there's a space you'd like to expand into—maybe you'd like to do more with estate planning or sustainable investing—a class or a new certification could help you jump-start that new area of your practice.

Principles of Continuous Education

Continuous education is a practical matter. You've got to find the time to take a class or build a new relationship. But it's also about your outlook and attitude. I believe an attitude of curiosity is invaluable in this business. The world of investing is always changing, and the only way to keep up is to stay curious.

Here are a few principles that shape my approach to continuous education:

Keep an open mind. It's important to avoid bias in this business. You have to stay politically neutral. You're going to have clients from across the political spectrum. Of course, you don't have to work with anyone whose views make you uncomfortable, but you should avoid prejudging people based on their political affiliations. I know what my politics are, and anyone can look up my political donations, but when I'm talking to clients, I'm always politically neutral.

It's also important to avoid bias when it comes to investing. Don't jump to conclusions about the impact of any election or other political event. If you look at history, the impact of any president on the market tends to be quite minimal. Presidential statements or other news stories might have a short-term implications, but over the long term markets are driven by earnings, interest rates, and liquidity more than any other factor.

Question assumptions. Political bias is just one example—any kind of bias or assumption could hold you back. It takes self-awareness to notice your own biases, but when you do catch yourself making a knee-jerk judgment about a stock, a sector, or a client, take time to step back and question your priors. Maybe there's more to the situation than you can see at a glance.

Don't believe everything you read. I believe in reading and educating yourself as much as possible. But you should question what you read too. There's plenty of commentary out there that just repeats unfounded assumptions. Especially these days, with social media, there's a ton of noise to sort through. And the twenty-four-hour news cycle means that commentary and analysis are coming out constantly. Remember that the first story on a breaking news event might not give you the complete picture. Whatever you read, take time to consider the source of the information. Does the outlet have an agenda or bias you need to take into account?

Know the difference between an opinion and a fact. Learn from your colleagues, especially people who are more experienced than you are. But question their biases and assumptions too. Don't let someone else's confidence sway you. Examine the evidence and draw your own conclusions.

Project confidence to clients. You can't know everything. But if a client asks you a question you don't know the answer to, the last thing you want to do is pretend you know. Say a client asks you about the outlook for titanium, and you really don't have a take. Stay calm, stay confident, and say something like, "That's really interesting. I know it's been doing well recently. Let me poke around and put together some research for you."

I had a client recently ask me about whether or not he should buy a physical shopping mall. I had a basic sense that there was a lot of uncertainty in the market, but I didn't know enough to give him a recommendation. So I said, "I'm going to get my analyst on the phone with you. She can give you a more in-depth look at what's happening in that market." The client's happy because he's getting the information he needs, and I'm providing great value because I'm connecting him to someone who eats, sleeps, and breathes shopping malls.

As an advisor, you should be a generalist. You should know at least a little bit about a lot of sectors. But what your clients really want is to feel confident that you can manage their money effectively. Remember: as overwhelming as the amount of information and noise is for you, it's far more overwhelming for your clients. The ability to bring order to that chaos is the hallmark of a good advisor.

You don't have to know everything. But you do need to project confidence. Carry yourself like you're an expert, and any information you don't happen to have at your fingertips you can easily find. The good news is that's true!

Key Takeaways

- Continuous education is essential because the investment world—and your clients—are ever changing.
- Set up a system to educate yourself.
- Everyone on the team needs to help educate everyone else.
- Professional networking is a must.
- Some principles of continuous education are key:
  - Keep an open mind.
  - Question your assumptions.
  - Don't believe everything you read.
  - Know the difference between opinion and fact.
  - Project confidence to your clients.

12

GETTING THROUGH CRISES

In the midst of every crisis, lies great opportunity.
—Albert Einstein

I've been in this business for a long time. And that means that I've seen a lot of corrections. Here's a brief list of market corrections I've been through in the course of my career:

- 1987: Black Monday
- 1989: October 13 minicrash
- 1990–1991: Recession
- 1991–1993: Savings and Loan Crisis
- 1991: Japanese Asset Bubble

- 1997: Asian Currency Crisis
- 2000–2002: Dot-Com Crash
- 2008–2009: The Great Financial Crisis
- 2010: European Debt Crisis
- 2011: US debt rating downgrade, August
- 2015: Chinese stock market crash
- 2016: Brexit
- 2018: Market sell-off due to fear of Fed hikes
- 2020: Global pandemic
- 2022: Higher inflation and interest rates

Some investors would look at this list and wonder how anyone could possibly have the guts to stay in the market through all these swings. But when I look at this list, I see opportunity.

Here's why: Over more than seventy years of market history, we have learned that market corrections are inevitable. Not only that, they happen with remarkable consistency. On average, markets decline 5 percent or more from peak to trough about three times a year, 10 percent or more once a year, 15 percent or more once every four years, and 20 percent or more once every six years. Between 2000 and 2019, a correction of at least 10 percent happened in eleven out of those twenty years.[13] That means a majority of years see at least a 10 percent market decline.

Even bear markets shouldn't frighten the long-term investor. The average bear market lasts less than eighteen months, and most corrections don't lead to true bear markets—a decline of 20 percent—anyway.[14]

Market corrections happen. You can't escape them. As an advisor, this spells opportunity for two reasons: First, most of the ordinary investors who are your clients don't have the perspective that you have. They are often frightened by market corrections. If you can step in and provide the historical context and offer calm, professional guidance, you have a huge opportunity to create new relationships during these periods, or cement existing relationships.

Second, corrections are typically great buying opportunities. On average, the S&P 500 tends to rise 8 percent a month after a correction, and 24 percent in the following year.[15] And even though the market saw a correction during a majority of the twenty years between 2000 and 2019, stocks still rose an average of 6 percent a year during that time.

Over the long term, stock markets have been an incredible source of wealth creation for people who have applied time-tested strategies of asset allocation and diversification. The short-term ride might be bumpy, but in the long term patient investors will profit. As a result, it often makes sense to buy into the market when assets are selling at a 5 or 10 percent discount.

---

13 David Koenig, "Market Corrections Are More Common Than You Might Think," Charles Schwab, February 25, 2022, https://intelligent.schwab.com/article/stock-market-corrections-not-uncommon.

14 Ibid.

15 Ibid.

I don't believe in trying to time the market. If you buy into a correction, you're just as likely to see some downside initially as you are to see an immediate gain. But again, over the long term, markets go up—twenty years from now, as long as you've bought a diversified range of assets that fit with your client's risk profile and long-term plan, you'll be glad you bought. The bottom line is, if you looked at every crisis as a buying opportunity, over the last thirty years, you would have been right every single time.

How to Help Clients through a Crisis

As an advisor, getting your clients through market corrections is a key part of your job. Let's walk through a five-step plan to ease the stress of a market correction for your clients.

1. Educate clients on market history. Nothing is more important than educating clients on market history. This should be a part of your new client onboarding process. In your initial conversations with a new client, you should ask questions to determine their risk tolerance and talk about their expectations for the money you're managing. If their expectations are out of line with market norms, it's crucial to talk them through how and why they're off base.

   Client education must include talking about corrections. Share a brief summation of the past thirty to fifty years of market history. Talk about how often corrections typically happen and give a brief preview of how you plan to handle corrections and what they can expect from you.

2. Reach out proactively when a correction begins. In March and April 2020, I spent my Saturdays and Sundays calling all my clients. I'd start each conversation by saying, "I wouldn't usually call you on a Saturday, but I wanted to let you know what's happening." Then I'd walk through the client's current asset allocation and talk about what we were seeing in terms of market moves and anything we might have been doing to rebalance their portfolios. Then, of course, I'd answer any questions that came up.

   A crisis is when your clients need you the most. In October 2009, I met a prospect who'd been referred to me by a mutual acquaintance. She actually reached out to us because her advisor had never called her when the market started to slide in response to the real estate crisis.

   I signed that client, and I've retained many others because I'm proactive during market corrections. I know my clients will be worried. The money they have invested with me isn't just money, after all—it's their ability to put their kids through college, their safety and security in retirement, their legacy. It's my job as their advisor to provide the perspective that will help them stick to their long-term plans, even when markets slide. In fact, touching base with clients during periods of volatility and market stress is probably a financial advisor's most important job.

   Your clients don't expect you to divine the future through a crystal ball. All they are looking for is a trustworthy partner who can help them navigate the gyrations of the market and make thoughtful and informed decisions. In the book *Chasing Positivity* by David Richman and Robert Brooks, they share the four Cs of client communication in turbulent markets: candor, clarity, commitment, and calm.

3. Stress test your clients' financial plans. Here's another way a correction can be an opportunity: it's an opportunity to run a real-world test on your clients' financial plans. It's a good idea to run through financial planning scenarios again during a correction to ensure that your clients are still on track to meet their goals, even if a correction turns into a true bear market. Hopefully these stress tests reveal that your clients' portfolios are doing exactly what they're supposed to do—provide reasonable long-term gains at a risk level the client is comfortable with.

   When the market falls 5, 10, or 15 percent, you may also discover something about a client's true risk tolerance. It's one thing to say you're comfortable with a short-term loss of 20 percent of your stock portfolio in the abstract, and another thing to actually live through it. If you find your clients are struggling to stick to their plans or obsessing about daily market noise, you might want to follow up after the worst of the crisis has passed and talk about some ways to derisk their portfolio.

4. Follow up with more education. During the pandemic, Merrill Lynch's chief investment officer came out with several prescient research reports we were able to share with our clients. We also shared other research and useful articles that we came across in our own reading. In regularly scheduled client calls, we discussed what we were learning about the pandemic's impact on the global economy and the markets and reinforced our previous conversations about the history of market corrections.

   Client education is not a one-time event. It should be an ongoing conversation. As an advisor, you can't control what happens in the market. But you can influence how your clients *feel* about market events. Education helps you guide your clients through volatility and keeps them focused on their long-term goals.

5. Share thought leadership to reach out to potential new clients. In addition to talking to existing clients, we take crises like the pandemic as an opportunity to help us connect with prospective clients. This outreach can be both general and specific. For example, we conducted four webinars over the pandemic year to share our perspective on economic trends. Those webinars helped us solidify existing relationships and generate new referrals. In the end, we collected over $200 million in new assets from this outreach.

   A crisis can also be an opportunity to reach out to a specific new prospect with material tailored to their interests. During the pandemic, we had a top prospect on our list who worked in the tourism business. As you can imagine, this was an incredibly stressful time for her. We reached out to her to share our research perspective on travel and tourism, and we signed her as a new client.

How My Clients and Colleagues Feel

It's easy for me to say I help my clients stay calm and stay focused on the long term. But my clients would say the same thing. Here's a few of the things my clients have said about working with me through market corrections:

- "I'm a nervous investor, so I tend to bug Raj all the time. But the thing that is so overwhelmingly impressive about him is how calm he can be in the middle of a storm. The market could be crashing down around him, and he's just even-keeled about it. He's an incredible sea of tranquility. It's like having the Rock of Gibraltar behind you. I see him as a guide to get me from point A to point Z. As the years go by, I value him more and more."

- "I'm not a risk-taker. I want to maintain my capital. I cannot tolerate losses, particularly now that I'm retired. Raj has always respected that and tailored my investments to my personality. He has a very calm personality."

- "I feel very well met with Raj. We can talk about things like the nature of risk. When the pandemic began, we talked about my portfolio, and we decided not to hedge as aggressively as we have in some past downturns. The comeback has been strong, but more importantly, he's always available to talk about my portfolio. Raj is always calm. He makes investing very approachable. He'll talk about what the assumptions are, what looks likely to happen, and why you would make certain moves. Markets are irrational, but they're not unknowable."

I'm thrilled that my clients see me this way, of course. This is exactly the kind of tone I'm trying to strike. But I would hope that any successful advisor would set the same tone when working with clients. This is one of the reasons it's so beneficial to work with an advisor in the first place: we can help clients step back and take the long view. While we care about our clients, we don't have as much emotionally on the line, and we can see the situation more objectively.

Of course, your calm and positive attitude must be genuine. Clients will be able to tell if you're panicking on the inside, even if you're telling them to stay the course.

I genuinely believe corrections are normal and that they typically spell opportunity. This isn't just something I tell clients to keep them from freaking out—it's how I speak to colleagues too. Here's a longtime colleague reflecting on one of the many crises we've lived through together: "In January 2009, I had just gotten a big promotion and was on my way to Boston. At the time, Bank of America was rumored to be going under. Its stock was selling at about three dollars. Most people were in end-of-the-world mode. But Raj said, 'We're on the brink of the biggest bull market of our careers.' He told me, 'When times are difficult, people are looking for leadership. They need advice. This is an opportunity like we've never seen.' He mentioned he had started out in the business in 1987, and all that turmoil actually propelled his career.

"Not only was he right about the market but he had this tremendous sense of optimism. No matter how difficult something is, he always looks at it as an opportunity. Raj not only looks at the glass as half full but his glass is overflowing."

That's what I believe—that's what I'll tell anyone who will listen. And as my colleague says, I've been proven right again and again. I've consistently found corrections and crises to be opportunities to buy at a discount and solidify client relationships.

The Case for Progress

Why am I so confident that patient investors will prosper in the long run? Well, for starters, it's been true historically. It's been true over the course of my career.

There will always be people who argue that this time is different. And it's true that each crisis proceeds differently. When it comes to recessions, every recovery is different too. Housing prices in some markets took more than ten years to recover from the Great Recession. After the recession of 2001, we had a "jobless recovery," in which economic growth rebounded, but hiring was slow. In 2008 the worst-hit industries offered mostly traditionally male-dominated jobs, like construction and manufacturing, leading some commentators to dub it a "mancession." The pandemic, on the other hand, led to a "shecession," in which many of the job losses were suffered by women. According to Pew Research, the recession resulted in a steep but brief contraction in employment, with greater job losses among women than men. Overall, the number of women ages 25 and older in the labor force has fallen 1.3% since the third quarter of 2019, similar to the 1.1% decline of men in the labor force.

Every crisis is different. The pain suffered by people who lose their jobs during a recession is obviously real. And every recovery is different. Sometimes the economy and employment rebound quickly, while other times progress is slow and halting. But over the long term, human ingenuity always prevails. And patient long-term investors always prosper.

As I write these words, we've just lived through yet another crisis—the crisis of the pandemic. In parts of the world, the worst of the crisis is very much still with us, while in other places we're seeing a halting but real recovery.

Despite the pandemic, I am hopeful and optimistic that humanity will progress in remarkable ways in the coming decades. That's been true throughout my career, and I believe it will continue to be true in the future. But don't take my word for it. Here's a brief reading list if you're not convinced:

In the book *Abundance*, authors Peter Diamandis and Steven Kotler write eloquently about the power of technology and innovation to enhance the lives of human beings on this planet.

In his book *Better Angels of Our Nature*, Harvard professor Steven Pinker demonstrates that we are now living in the most peaceful time in human history, despite the daily barrage of bad news.

In his seminal work *Factfulness*, the great Swedish thinker and public health expert Hans Rosling writes about the ten reasons why we are wrong about the world and lucidly details the incredible progress we have made in enhancing the lives of people around the world.

There's no denying that we face enormous challenges. For example, the transition to a sustainable economy that we are already living through and that will continue to be a major driver of economic and cultural change over the next decades will undoubtedly cause some corrections in the years to come. But over the long term, I believe humans will continue to solve big problems and make life better for everyone on this planet. And that's reason for optimism.

Key Takeaways

- There have been many financial crises during my career, beginning in 1987.

- The way to understand a crisis is to see it as an investment opportunity.
- To get through a crisis with your clients, educate them on financial history.
- Reach out proactively when the crisis starts.
- Stress test client plans during the crisis.
- Commit to continuous education of your clients.
- Share thought leadership with prospective clients to win new clients during downturns.

13

THE GREAT WEALTH TRANSFER

Sixty-eight trillion dollars.

Over the next twenty to thirty years, baby boomers will begin transferring their accumulated wealth to their children. This "Great Wealth Transfer" is estimated to add up to $68 trillion dollars owned by about forty-five million households.[16] It's a massive trend that will reshape almost everything about the financial planning business, and it has the potential to dramatically change the economic environment too. If you're a young advisor just starting out in the business, this trend will shape the next thirty years of your career, so it's wise to learn as much as you can about how to prepare

16 Kate Dore, "Are you prepared for tax impact of the $68 trillion great wealth transfer? Here are some options to reduce the bite," CNBC, July 12, 2021, https://www.cnbc.com/2021/07/12/the-great-wealth-transfer-has-a-big-tax-impact-how-to-reduce-the-bite.html?__source=iosappshare%7Ccom.apple.UIKit.activity.Mail.

to help clients in both older and younger generations manage this massive change.

The driving forces behind the Great Wealth Transfer are relatively simple. Baby boomers currently own the majority of the wealth in America—53 percent compared to 17 percent for the silent generation, 25 percent for Generation X, and just under 5 percent for millennials.[17] In part, that's because boomers have had longer to save and accumulate assets. But it's also worth noting that millennials are worse off financially now than their boomer parents were at their age.

There's no single reason for the difference between the financial trajectory of the boomer generation and their children. Many millennials had the bad luck to graduate college during or in the aftermath of the Great Recession. They also accumulated more educational debt than their parents did, as college costs have risen astronomically in the past few decades. Wages have also grown very slowly in the past forty years. In short, millennials are a financially strapped generation, with more debt and less in savings than their parents have now or had at their age.

As the boomers begin to transfer their wealth to their children in the next few decades, the Great Wealth Transfer will shape the landscape in which financial planners are operating in several key ways. Let's look at three major impacts of the Great Wealth Transfer in turn.

---

17 Alicia Adamczyk, "Millennials own less than 5% of all U.S. wealth," CNBC, October 9, 2020, https://www.cnbc.com/2020/10/09/millennials-own-less-than-5percent-of-all-us-wealth.html.

1. Estate planning and the logistics of the actual transfer will be crucial needs. There's a reason my team and I have pushed hard to develop our expertise on estate planning. Our clients are already aging, and as the Great Wealth Transfer picks up steam, this trend will only grow.

To succeed in this environment, financial planners must have a firm grasp on the major strategies for passing on wealth to the next generation. They must also stay relatively up to speed on changes in tax law, as these can have a major impact on how clients are best advised to accomplish the transfer of their wealth.

There are many decisions for clients to make. Do they want to give some money to their children and grandchildren during their lifetime, or accomplish everything through estate planning? Do they want to set up 529 plans for any younger family members' educations? What actual instruments are best? Should they establish a trust or make their children the beneficiaries of their retirement accounts or life insurance policies? How much charitable giving do they want to do?

Clients will also need to consider the dynamics within their families as they prepare for these transfers. How good are their children at managing money? What can they do to help ensure that the money is spent responsibly? Should they simply leave those decisions up to the next generation?

Financial advisors can also play an important role in helping their aging clients plan for their late-in-life care needs. Nursing home care, if needed, can be far more expensive than many people realize. Financial plans should take this possibility into account. And family dynamics come into play here too. The best financial advisors will talk to aging parents and their adult children about how the family will decide when parents should no longer be managing their own financial affairs and who will take over power of attorney at that time.

2. Millennials will become the clients of the future. As the Great Wealth Transfer begins, some advisors who've been working with aging clients for many years will either take on their clients' children as clients or lose those assets.

   That's one reason my team and I have put a lot of effort into deepening our relationships not just with our clients but with our clients' families. Through our work on estate planning, philanthropy, and family dynamics, we're getting to know our clients' kids. As I've mentioned, we often provide extra services to families, like best practices on prenups or career advice, that help us make that connection with the next generation.

   But if you're a young advisor who's just starting out, this wealth transfer could become an advantage for you. Research suggests that as many as 80 percent of millennials who inherit money from their parents will look for new advisors rather than sticking with their parents' financial planners.[18] If you are a millennial yourself, you can probably relate better to millennial clients than an old guy like me.

   As a demographic group, millennials are more diverse, more educated, and more progressive than previous gener-

18 Andrew Osterland, "What the coming $68 trillion Great Wealth Transfer means for financial advisors," CNBC, October 21, 2019, https://www.cnbc.com/2019/10/21/what-the-68-trillion-great-wealth-transfer-means-for-advisors.html.

ations.[19] They tend to marry later and have children later, changing the way they approach parenting and providing for a family. They're also more likely to be living with a romantic partner but not married.[20]

When it comes to their values, millennials are much more focused on climate change than previous generations: 71 percent of them say climate action should be a top priority.[21] They have more favorable views of foreign countries and international organizations than older generations do, and they're less likely to believe that America is exceptional.[22] We'll dis-

19 Kristen Bialik and Richard Fry, "Millennial life: How young adulthood today compares with prior generations," Pew Research Center, February 14, 2019, https://www.pewresearch.org/social-trends/2019/02/14/millennial-life-how-young-adulthood-today-compares-with-prior-generations-2/.

20 Amanda Barroso, Kim Parker, and Jesse Bennett, "As Millennials Near 40, They're Approaching Family Life Differently Than Previous Generations," Pew Research Center, May 27, 2020, https://www.pewresearch.org/social-trends/2020/05/27/as-millennials-near-40-theyre-approaching-family-life-differently-than-previous-generations/.

21 Alec Tyson, Brian Kennedy, and Cary Funk, "Gen Z, Millennials Stand Out for Climate Change Activism, Social Media Engagement With Issue," Pew Research Center, May 26, 2020, https://www.pewresearch.org/science/2021/05/26/gen-z-millennials-stand-out-for-climate-change-activism-social-media-engagement-with-issue/.

22 Christine Huang and Laura Silver, "U.S. Millennials tend to have favorable views of foreign countries and institutions – even as they age," Pew Research Center, July 8, 2020, https://www.pewresearch.org/fact-tank/2020/07/08/u-s-millennials-tend-to-have-favorable-views-of-foreign-countries-and-institutions-even-as-they-age/.

cuss some of the implications of these values for millennials' financial choices in succeeding chapters. For now, it's enough to say that financial advisors should have a good read on their clients' values and should shape financial plans accordingly. That's one of many reasons I approach discovery sessions with such care, and why I try to ask open-ended questions and really let clients speak. I want to get to know my clients, their goals, and priorities in order to design a financial plan that will suit them.

Advisors working with millennials will also need to understand the way their financial situations are different from previous generations. Again, if you're a younger advisor who's just coming up in the business, you might have dealt with some of millennials' most pressing financial issues in your own life. As mentioned above, millennials have less in savings and more outstanding debt than their parents did at their age. Many of them are behind in saving for retirement and still paying off significant student loans. They're less likely to own a house than previous generations were at their age, and because they're starting families later, paying for their kids' college will come closer to their own retirement than it did for earlier generations.

For advisors who've been working with baby boomers for a long time, this will be a big adjustment. A typical millennial who's inheriting money from their parents will have more on their mind than just asset allocation. They'll want to know how they should prioritize paying off debt, saving for retirement, and saving for their kids' college expenses. Advisors should be prepared with their own takes on these questions, but they should also be prepared to listen and learn about their clients' personal priorities.

Millennial clients will also have different expectations in terms of *how* they work with their advisors. Millennials are the first generation of digital natives. Where their parents balanced their checkbooks on paper and called their advisors on the phone, millennials are used to checking their account balances online and, if they're invested in the stock market at all, making trades on their own, online. Millennials are twice as likely as boomers to use a robo-advisor to manage their investments automatically.[23] Financial advisors who want to capture their business will have to make it easy for them to monitor their accounts online and communicate digitally, where regulations allow.

Advisors may also have to work harder to convince millennial clients that they're providing real value that a robo-advisor can't. That means investing even more time in client relationships—in client education, in personalized financial planning, in proactive communication around market crises, and so on. A high-touch personalized approach will help advisors set themselves apart from digital tools for money management, which tend to be more one-size-fits-all.

Above all, advisors of any age who are helping to manage the Great Wealth Transfer for their clients will need to maintain good relationships with both generations. Whether the parents or the children are your primary client, you'll have a

23 Nathaniel Lee, "Why robo-advisors are striving toward a 'hybrid model,' as the industry passes the $460 billion mark," CNBC, April 12, 2021, https://www.cnbc.com/2021/04/12/why-robo-advisors-may-never-replace-human-financial-advisors.html.

better long-term relationship with the client if you're able to speak to all members of the family.

This can be a challenge. Even in close families that get along well, parents and children can have different priorities. Baby boomer parents feel they've worked hard their entire lives to accumulate these assets, and they might want some sense of control or influence over how the money will be spent. Meanwhile, many millennials feel like their parents don't fully understand what the economic landscape is like for their generation. Helping families navigate these dynamics can be an invaluable service for an advisor to provide.

3. Advisors themselves are aging. The average financial advisor's client is sixty-five years old. The average financial advisor is sixty-one.[24] Even as baby boomer clients are transitioning to retirement and making their estate plans, millions of advisors are also nearing retirement age.

   The smart advisors of my generation are making clear succession plans and communicating those plans to their clients. A client who's about my age doesn't want to feel like I'm going to retire and leave them in the lurch just when they're starting to worry about whether their assets will produce enough income for them to live comfortably in retirement, or when a health issue comes up that forces them to adjust their plans. A younger client definitely doesn't want to have to search for a new advisor when I retire, given that they'll still need decades

---

24 Steve Gresham, "The Other, Bigger Wealth Transfer," *Financial Advisor*, June 1, 2021, https://www.fa-mag.com/news/the-other--bigger-wealth-transfer-62308.html.

of retirement planning and money management.

I'm being very proactive about sharing my succession plans with my clients and making sure they get to know the younger members of my team so that they can feel comfortable that they're in good hands even after I step back from the day-to-day business. But effective succession planning isn't just about letting clients know who will take over when I retire. It's also about preparing those younger team members to take on the responsibility.

The fact that so many advisors are part of my generation creates a huge opportunity for younger advisors. If I were just starting out right now, I'd be looking for older advisors whose careers I admire. I'd be seeking them out for informational interviews, asking their advice on how to build a business, and bringing them "big fish" clients I might not be able to land on my own.

Building relationships deliberately with older advisors now could have multiple benefits. Of course, you get the benefit of the advice and mentorship now. As discussed in an previous chapter, partnering with an older, more experienced advisor can help you land a higher caliber of client. You can get experience working with larger or more complicated portfolios while you have that older advisor around to reassure the client they're in good hands and to help you learn the ropes.

I wouldn't necessarily ask an older advisor when they're planning to retire or whether you can be a part of their succession plans. But building relationships certainly can't hurt, and it could put you in a good position to take over with some of your mentor's clients down the road.

Will the Pandemic Affect the Great Wealth Transfer?

During the housing crisis and market crash of 2008, there were lots of worried news reports about people who were near retirement and had suddenly lost 20–25 percent of the investments they had hoped would support them during retirement. There was a particular focus on target-date funds,[25] a type of mutual fund that's designed to automatically do the kind of portfolio rebalancing a good advisor would do, gradually derisking the portfolio and shifting from an all-stock allocation to a more conservative mix of stocks and bonds as the "target" retirement date approaches.

Today, of course, we're living through another major crisis. And while good advisors and savvy investors know market crises happen and don't change the long-term benefit of investing, it's natural for people who are close to retirement to worry about how a major stock market decline will affect their financial plans. Right now, because we are on the cusp of this Great Wealth Transfer, older and younger adults might wonder how the pandemic will affect boomers' financial plans.

The first thing to note is that the stock market has already rebounded and more than made up for the losses we saw early in the pandemic. So disciplined investors who stuck to their long-term plans should have seen a temporary dip in their accounts, followed by significant gains.

This raises another point: while major losses right around retirement can be nerve-racking, it is appropriate for someone

25 Darla Mercado, "These 401(k) funds took a beating in 2008—and it could happen again," CNBC, September 14, 2018, https://www.cnbc.com/2018/09/13/these-retirement-funds-took-a-beating-in-2008-it-could-happen-again.html.

at retirement age to still be invested in stocks and other higher-reward assets, such as private equity. The average person retires at age sixty-four.[26] The average life expectancy in the United States is seventy-nine.[27] More than half of women and a third of men can expect to live significantly longer than that, and someone who lives to be eighty has good odds of celebrating a ninetieth birthday, as well.[28] A person in good health who retires at sixty-five should have a financial plan that will support their lifestyle for another twenty-five or thirty years at least, as well as prepare them for late-in-life health-care expenses. A responsible financial plan can't move all assets into low-risk, low-return investments at retirement, because the client would lose too much ground to inflation.

The one factor that could make this crisis different is the timing of boomers' retirement. About 10 percent of boomers have retired early due to the pandemic.[29] For some, the risks of going into an office or being around people simply seemed too great. For others, the strong stock market rebound and rising home prices made retiring earlier than planned financially viable.[30] Others, especially

26 John Csiszar, "The Average Retirement Age in Every State," Yahoo!, July 4, 2021, https://www.yahoo.com/now/average-retirement-age-every-state-160000077.html.

27 "Life Expectancy," CDC, https://www.cdc.gov/nchs/fastats/life-expectancy.htm.

28 K. G. Manton and J. W. Vaupel, "Survival after the age of 80 in the United States, Sweden, France, England, and Japan," *New England Journal of Medicine*, 333, no. 18 (November 1995): 1232–5.

29 Stephanie Asymkos, "Pandemic led to early retirement for many Americans—some voluntary, some not," Yahoo!, June 12, 2021, https://money.yahoo.com/pandemic-led-to-early-retirement-for-many-americans-152011747.html.

30 https://www.nytimes.com/2021/07/02/business/economy/retire-early-pandemic-social-security.html

lower-income boomers, lost their jobs or saw small businesses flounder and were essentially forced into an early retirement. And some simply took the pandemic as a time for reflection and decided they were ready to spend more time with family.

Whatever the reason for early retirement, it does have a major impact on financial plans. Financial advisors with older clients should be working with them to ensure that changing their retirement plans doesn't throw their financial plans off track.

Ultimately, the amount of wealth the baby boomer generation holds as a whole is so large that even a major crisis like the pandemic won't change the overall trajectory of the coming wealth transfer. But life changes for individual clients could have major effects on their particular plans, including their estate plans. Of course, that's where a good advisor can be invaluable in helping make sure their clients' legacies are secure.

Key Takeaways

- Baby boomers will transfer $68 trillion dollars to succeeding generations in the next few decades.
- Millennials have different financial needs and values than baby boomers.
- Estate planning will be key.
- It's important to understand the differing needs and perspectives of the generations and plan accordingly.

- To keep your business strong, you should have a succession plan yourself and prepare your clients for the handoff to younger advisors.

14

ENVIRONMENTAL, SOCIAL, AND GOVERNANCE (ESG)

Sustainable investing is not an all-or-nothing proposition.
—Jackie VanderBrug

I recently sat down with the daughter of one of my clients. When her parents pass, she will inherit about $20 million. We've tried over the years to build a relationship with her in hopes of keeping her business after the family wealth transfers to the next generation. I believe we'll succeed—in part because we are listening and working to understand who she is, independent of who her parents are.

At our latest meeting, this woman told me that she's passionate about investing according to her values. She wants to design a portfolio that cuts out fossil fuels, guns, and other types of investment she's morally opposed to. She wants to favor companies that prioritize diversity, promote women, and are well governed and run for the benefit of employees, shareholders, and the communities around them, not focused on short-term profit alone.

"For me," she told me, "this is a must-do, not a nice-to-do. I don't care if it limits my returns. I'm raising my kids with a certain set of values, and I need to put my money where my mouth is."

This woman is not alone. Particularly in the younger generations, I'm seeing a growing number of investors interested in aligning their portfolios with what are known as ESG investing principles—environmental, social, and corporate governance metrics. And as this woman's story illustrates, ESG investing is becoming a priority even for very wealthy families. The upcoming generations of wealth are not interested in maximizing their own profits at the expense of the natural world, human rights, or public health. Their values are important to them, and they want their investing to do good in the world, even as it benefits their personal bottom line.

ESG Investing Is a Growing Trend

The statistics are astounding. ESG funds captured $51 billion in new assets just in 2020, for a fifth consecutive record-breaking year of growth.[31] In fact, these funds drew in more than double the new money in 2020 that they captured in 2019. ESG investing is not just growing but it's growing at an accelerating rate—and increasingly becoming a mainstream strategy. In August 2021, the CEO

31 Greg Iacurci, "Money invested in ESG funds more than doubles in a year," CNBC, February 11, 2021, https://www.cnbc.com/2021/02/11/sustainable-investment-funds-more-than-doubled-in-2020-.html.

of the S&P Dow Jones Indices said the firm was "treating ESG as one of our biggest growth opportunities."[32]

About a quarter of all the money that flowed into mutual funds in 2020 went to ESG funds that limit their investments to companies that meet certain environmental, social, or corporate governance-related metrics.

That growth is only expected to grow. By 2030, assets in ESG investments could reach $1 trillion.[33] That would represent an eightfold increase from 2020.[34] Their growth in 2021 is already outpacing the record-setting growth of 2020.

The trend also isn't limited to smaller investors who invest directly in mutual funds. ESG investing now accounts for about a third of the money managed by professional asset managers in the United States.[35] Sustainable and socially responsible investing

---

32 Lizzy Gurdus, "ESG is one of our biggest growth opportunities, S&P Dow Jones CEO says," CNBC, August 21, 2021, https://www.cnbc.com/2021/08/21/esg-is-one-of-our-biggest-growth-opportunities-sp-dow-jones-ceo.html?__source=iosappshare%7Ccom.apple.UIKit.activity.Mail.

33 Lizzy Gurdus, "ESG investing to reach $1 trillion by 2030, says head of iShares Americas as carbon transition funds launch," CNBC, May 9, 2021, https://www.cnbc.com/2021/05/09/esg-investing-to-reach-1-trillion-by-2030-head-of-ishares-americas.html.

34 "ESG Investing: The Time is Now," State Street Global Advisors Funds Distributors, 2020, https://spdrs.emiclients.com/shared/pdfs/1816/esg-investing-infographic.pdf.

35 Debbie Carlson, "ESG investing now accounts for one-third of total U.S. assets under management," MarketWatch, November 17, 2020, https://www.marketwatch.com/story/esg-investing-now-accounts-for-one-third-of-total-u-s-assets-under-management-11605626611.

by professional money managers has been growing an average of 14 percent per year since 1995, with the fastest growth happening since 2012.

There are a number of factors driving this trend. One is simple logistics—more money is flowing into ESG strategies because more funds and ETFs are being created that make these strategies accessible to ordinary investors. Professional money managers and high-net-worth individuals have been able to design customized portfolios for some time, but as ETFs make these strategies mainstream, momentum continues to grow.

Millennials and younger generations are also big drivers of this trend. They're facing a set of existential issues that are more urgent than those faced by previous generations: climate change is reaching a critical phase, geopolitics have become more unstable, and global pandemics once only imagined are now a reality. Younger investors are much more passionate about environmental causes in particular than their parents were, and they're more willing to shape their investments to match their values. The Great Wealth Transfer we discussed in the previous chapter will only intensify the ESG trend as millennials inherit their parents' wealth and put it to work in ESG strategies they're already familiar with.

Climate change is the biggest single issue driving ESG investing. Investing with a focus on climate change and sustainability can include both avoiding fossil fuel stocks and seeking out renewable energy stocks or other investments that could benefit from a transition to a greener economy. That means there's both a push and a pull driving individuals and institutions toward sustainable investing. On the more activist side, there's a vocal and growing divestment movement that's pressuring large institutional investors to pull their money out of fossil fuels. Activists claim that institutions representing well over $11 trillion have committed to blacklist all fossil fuel investments.[36]

The pandemic year brought even more investor attention to ESG issues. The disruption of the pandemic brought issues of poverty, worker rights, and the wealth gap into sharper focus. Protests throughout the summer renewed activists' focus on racial equity. And the growing threat of wildfires in the West and the steady drumbeat of news about floods, storms, and extreme heat have made the climate crisis feel increasingly urgent for mainstream consumers and investors.

In my own practice, I'm already seeing a rapid evolution in ESG investing. ESG investing is no longer about simply selecting a fund that screens out a few blacklisted asset classes and calling it a day. My clients are increasingly interested in more and more granular targeting of their investments. When they invest, they're thinking about issues like women's inclusion, human rights, animal welfare, sustainable farming, alternative energy, LGBTQ+ awareness, global bondage and slavery, and several other trends.

The growth of ESG reminds me of the introduction of asset base pricing in the 1990s. Advisors who fail to understand and embrace the ESG paradigm risk losing market share and clients. In the nineties, many senior advisors resisted asset-based pricing and clung to the commission-based transaction model. Unfortunately, many of them stopped growing their practices or even exited the industry because they were reluctant to embrace change. The same could happen today to advisors who refuse to embrace ESG investing.

---

36 "Global Fossil Fuel Divestment and Clean Energy Investment Movement Crosses $11 Trillion Milestone," 350, September 9, 2019, https://350.org/press-release/global-fossil-fuel-divestment-11t/.

It's Not about Giving Up Alpha

I know some financial advisors pooh-pooh ESG investing. They believe it's something to do with a small fraction of a portfolio. They're stuck in an old mindset in which a focus on sustainability, social impact, and corporate governance means giving up some returns in exchange for a warm fuzzy feeling. Ultimately, they think most investors aren't willing to shave points off the bottom line just to make themselves feel better about their impact on the world.

This is an outdated mindset. Companies that are bad actors may profit in the short term, but over the long term, well-run companies that have a positive impact on the world will win out. And that's not just my opinion—there's a growing body of evidence that ESG funds outperform in the long run.

The majority of sustainable investing funds outperformed conventional funds from 2010–2020, for example.[37] When you dig into the details, the performance for stock-focused sustainable funds is even stronger—80 percent of US large-cap equity funds with a sustainable screen outperformed conventional large-cap stock funds, according to a Morningstar study. Morningstar researchers note that companies that meet ESG criteria tend to have healthier balance sheets and lower volatility than the average company.[38] This suggests that ESG investing is not only good for returns in the long term but it can also contribute to a better, more comfortable investor experience.

---

37 https://www.ft.com/content/733ee6ff-446e-4f8b-86b2-19ef42da3824

38 Dan Lefkovitz, "ESG Investing Performance Analyzed," Morningstar, March 12, 2019, https://www.morningstar.com/insights/2019/03/12/esg-investing-perfor_0.

ESG funds particularly stood out during the stock market swings caused by the pandemic. ESG funds outperformed the S&P 500 during the pandemic, avoiding some losses that were driven by oil and gas stocks, and gaining more during the rebound than the broader index.[39] Of course, the pandemic was a special circumstance. But the evidence is growing that the idea that sustainable investing means giving up returns is nothing more than a myth.

In fact, many analysts believe ESG investing will actually add alpha. Al Gore recently declared that advisors who don't adapt to ESG trends "are in serious danger of violating their fiduciary responsibility to their clients by leaving money on the table."[40] Of course, Gore has an agenda. But impartial observers are starting to seriously consider the same argument.

For one thing, as ESG investing grows in popularity, it can also become something of a self-fulfilling prophecy. If more and more institutional and individual investors are avoiding fossil fuel stocks, for example, there will simply be fewer buyers for those stocks. Increasing flows into ESG funds also support the prices of those funds.

In the longer term, some analysts believe ESG investing will bring higher returns because of the greater care companies have to

39 Will Feuer, "Here's More Evidence That ESG Funds Outperformed During the Pandemic," *Institutional Investor*, April 7, 2021, https://www.institutionalinvestor.com/article/b1r9gb5p9k10b4/Here-s-More-Evidence-That-ESG-Funds-Outperformed-During-the-Pandemic.

40 Gillian Tett, "Why ESG investing makes fund managers more money," *Financial Times*, July 9, 2020, https://www.ft.com/content/1cfb5e02-7ce1-4020-9c7c-624a3dd6ead9.

take to meet ESG criteria.[41] To get past an ESG screen, companies typically have to audit their supply chains. There's some evidence that a deep dive into supplier logistics helped Walmart, for example, better weather the intense challenges of the pandemic.

A Crucial Area of Study for Advisors

I'm not here to give you investing advice. As an advisor, you have to do your own research and come to your own conclusions. But based on what I've seen as this trend has grown, I believe ESG investing is a crucial area for advisors to at least be knowledgeable about.

Today ESG might be a trend, but tomorrow it will be a tsunami. It is incumbent on advisors to keep an open mind and understand the forces shaping and impacting ESG investing. The ability to discuss this subject with clients and prospects will determine how successful you will be in gathering assets and establishing your thought leadership. This is not an area that should be delegated to a specialist. It is an essential field of study for every advisor.

ESG investing is not a short-term trend. It's about that generational changing of the guard, and it reflects changing attitudes toward money. Increasingly, younger generations are rejecting the idea that making money and doing good are separate activities—that you put your money to work with no other consideration than seeking alpha, and you volunteer for good causes in your free time or make tax-deductible donations to charity at the end of the year. Younger investors want their money to have a positive impact on the world.

41 Ibid.

You can see this sea change in the rise of B Corporations organized to pursue a "double bottom line" of both positive impact and profit. You can see it in the growing consumer demand for more sustainable products, fair-trade products, and other brands that are seen as having a positive impact on the world. Both institutional and retail investors are also becoming more likely to launch or support activist campaigns to hold management to account and pursue ESG-related goals.[42] ESG investing is part of a larger wave of social change, and it's not going away anytime soon.

New Trends in ESG Investing

The past ten years have been about the rapid growth of ESG investing as a trend. But as I mentioned, I'm already seeing the demand from my clients for more detailed and granular approach to sustainable investing. As ESG investing matures, it will continue to evolve and change, and advisors should continue to stay on top of these trends. Over the next couple of decades, here are three major ESG investing trends analysts suggest watching out for:

1. Better, more detailed data. As ESG investing grows, it will become less of a blunt instrument and more of a scalpel. Large institutional investors are increasingly putting pressure on companies to disclose, in detail, their plans for achieving net-zero emissions.[43]

42 Bruce H. Goldfarb and Alexandra Higgins, "Shareholder Activists Gear Up for a Busy 2021 – With New Tools and Tactics," Harvard Law School Forum on Corporate Governance, April 14, 2022, https://corpgov.law.harvard.edu/.

43 Martina Cheung, "Seven ESG Trends to Watch in 2021," S&P Global, February 8, 2021, https://www.spglobal.com/en/research-insights/featured/seven-esg-

New regulations in the EU are pushing companies to disclose more detailed information about ESG issues, and the SEC is considering new rules about when and how companies must disclose risks they face from climate change.[44] Investors interested in sustainability and other ESG issues will be able to dive into more and more detail as more data is made available. Some analysts also believe artificial intelligence could play a role in analyzing and making predictions around companies' performance as compared to their ESG risks.[45]

2. More political pressure on climate. The Biden administration, and new net-zero policies around the world, will increase the political pressure on companies to take more effective action on climate. Look for more urgency in discussions around biodiversity loss, the transition to a net-zero economy, and climate resilience.[46]

3. Greater focus on social issues, particularly diversity. Diversity has always been a part of ESG discussions, but the protests following the murder of George Floyd brought renewed attention to racial equity issues in the United States and around the world. Investors are also starting to look beyond the simplest measures of diversity and pushing for more detailed information. Increasingly,

---

trends-to-watch-in-2021.

44 Allison Herren Lee, "Public Input Welcomed on Climate Change Disclosures," US Securities and Exchange Commission, March 15, 2021, https://www.sec.gov/news/public-statement/lee-climate-change-disclosures.

45 Kosmas Papadopoulos and Rodolfo Araujo, "Top 10 ESG Trends for the New Decade," Harvard Law School Forum on Corporate Governance, April 14, 2022, https://corpgov.law.harvard.edu/.

46 Martina Cheung, "Seven ESG Trends to Watch in 2021," S&P Global, February 8, 2021, https://www.spglobal.com/en/research-insights/featured/seven-esg-trends-to-watch-in-2021.

investors want to see not just data on gender ratios but on race and sexual orientation too.[47] And investors are looking beyond the makeup of the board to press for information on a company's entire workforce.[48]

Where a Professional Advisor Can Add Value

Off-the-shelf ESG funds often paint with a pretty broad brush. Ratings firms assign companies an ESG rating based on how much the company appears to be at risk from ESG factors and funds screen based on those ratings.[49] Phillip Morris, for example, makes the cut for the Dow Jones Sustainability Index, but might not satisfy many investors' definition of a *socially responsible company*. Other companies, like Amazon or Facebook, may satisfy ESG criteria in terms of their carbon footprint, but might make some socially conscious investors uncomfortable due to their labor policies or larger impact on the social sphere.

An individual investor on their own has to choose an off-the-shelf solution. They'll have to do their own research on how each fund determines which companies make the cut. And they'll have to try to figure out on their own which ESG-related factors are

---

47 Ibid.

48 Kosmas Papadopoulos and Rodolfo Araujo, "Top 10 ESG Trends for the New Decade," Harvard Law School Forum on Corporate Governance, April 14, 2022, https://corpgov.law.harvard.edu/.

49 Hans Taparia, "The World May Be Better Off Without ESG Investing," *Stanford Social Innovation Review*, July 14, 2021, https://ssir.org/articles/entry/the_world_may_be_better_off_without_esg_investing#.

most important to them and which are most likely to impact performance either positively or negatively.

An advisor can play an invaluable role in helping investors sort through their options when it comes to ESG investing. And particularly for high-net-worth individuals, advisors can design customized portfolios that will adhere to the individual client's values while also providing a diversified mix of assets that suit the client's risk profile and long-term goals.

I also believe advisors should be providing thought leadership on this topic to all their clients and prospective clients. Even investors who aren't interested in ESG investing in their own portfolios will appreciate having an advisor who is up-to-date on market trends and has a perspective to offer. And investors who do want to align their investing with their values will be drawn to advisors who are out in front on this issue, who have a clear take on which strategies work best to combine rigorous values-based screens with the potential for strong long-term returns, and who are able to design customized portfolios that take ESG trends into account.

Our firm has deep resources in ESG, and we have made it an essential part of our investment process. I make sure to share thought leadership pieces on ESG investing with clients and review its importance at every review call or meeting. My goal is to make them aware of our team's commitment and capabilities in this area.

Recently, I received a nice referral from a client to the trustees of a family foundation that was seeking advisors who understood the ESG space. We won the mandate after two meetings and secured a new $25 million relationship! All we did was plant a seed in the client's mind that we were active in this emerging segment.

We have tremendous resources available to share with any clients who are interested in ESG investing. But purpose, impact, and legacy are key parts of the discussions we have with all clients. In a competitive market, it's better to have a distinct point of view than to try to be all things to all people. We are serious, long-term investors who believe wealth has a purpose and should be put to work doing good in the world—that's our brand. I believe that brand will continue to attract thoughtful, purposeful clients for years to come.

Key Takeaways

- The younger generation of investors are very interested in ESG investing.
- ESG investor numbers are accordingly growing rapidly.
- The driving issue is climate change.
- ESG investing can't be ignored and needs to be part of every financial advisor's tool kit.

15

FAMILY DYNAMICS

True wealth is not measured in money or status or power. It is measured in the legacy we leave behind for those we love and those we inspire.
—Cesar Chavez

I arrived in America in the fall of 1980. My dad was hale and hearty when I left India. Two months later, he died of a heart attack. He was only fifty-nine years old.

My dad's death shook my world. I was in my early twenties, and suddenly I felt responsible for helping to raise my younger brothers, who were thirteen and sixteen, and taking care of my mother. My mother hadn't worked full time for a long time by that point. My dad had given me money for my first semester at college, but we'd never talked about how much he had in savings or anything like that.

I called up my dad's business partner to ask him about making some arrangements for my education and for the rest of the family. He basically told me there was no money available. My dad had put everything into his business, and business had been tough.

I had gone from feeling like everything was taken care of to realizing that everything was falling on my shoulders. It was a shock on top of a terrible shock.

The sad truth is that stories like this are all too common. Talking about money is taboo in many cultures, for many reasons. In some families, the "head of the household"—often a man—sees it as a matter of pride and duty to handle money matters alone. In others, parents are afraid that being too open about how much money they truly have will turn their children into spoiled brats. Some families don't talk about money, because they feel ashamed they don't have much. Others avoid the topic because they don't want to call attention to their wealth.

Of course, the clients I work with tend to be high-net-worth individuals and families. My clients typically know they need to teach their children how to manage wealth. And yet because most of my clients are first-generation wealth creators, they usually don't have a model of *how* to do this kind of financial education with their kids or other heirs. Their parents may have taught them how to make a budget, stressed the importance of saving, or shared other important financial lessons, but they weren't brought up to work with financial advisors, to manage a trust worth multiple millions of dollars, or to find purpose in their lives once they no longer need to earn a salary to survive. They want to teach the next generation to manage wealth responsibly, but they aren't sure how.

That's where my team and I come in.

Over the past three decades, the role of financial advisors has changed dramatically. In the eighties, advisors were called stockbrokers and were purely transactional. In the nineties, asset-based pricing led to better portfolio construction and the use of more robust financial planning models. We were then called registered representatives. In the early part of this century, formal financial planning started to take hold—retirement analysis, college funding, and estate planning. This new shift in the financial advisor's role led to the new moniker wealth management advisor.

Today the business is more sophisticated and professional than it has ever been. To build a successful career as an advisor, you need to embrace holistic financial planning, integrated portfolio management, estate and tax strategy, liability management, insurance, risk management, and philanthropy. The most common title today for advisors working with high-net-worth families is private wealth advisor.

In my opinion, the emerging new frontier for advisors is family dynamics. This field encompasses a wide spectrum of areas: clarifying family values and defining the purpose of wealth, setting a framework and rules for financial engagement within a family, cultivating a sense of ownership and accountability, developing financial self-reliance, infusing a sense of purpose through philanthropy, embracing socially responsible investing, and developing a collaborative advisory relationship. You are no longer just a financial or wealth advisor—you are truly a life advisor, and your goal is to help families sustain wealth through generations and guide them with purpose and intention to accomplish meaningful goals.

To be effective in this new field, you need to develop a whole set of new skills—you need to master the new language of family dynamics, become a better communicator, and understand the best practices of some of the most successful families in the world.

Let's walk through a few of the major ways financial advisors can be helpful to high-net-worth families in learning to navigate the world of wealth, preparing the next generation for the responsibilities, and developing a sense of purpose.

Family Values and the Purpose of Wealth

This is a top-of-mind concern for a lot of my wealthy clients. Remember: I tend to work with wealth creators. These are entrepreneurs and other high achievers who weren't raised with wealth. They've worked hard all their lives, and in many cases they defined themselves through their work. They have a lot of concerns about how their children will react to growing up with such a different reality. Will they develop a strong work ethic if they don't *have* to work? Will they learn to manage money responsibly if they have a large enough cushion to catch them every time they fall? Will they end up spoiled or unaware of their own privilege?

In general, Americans' financial literacy is quite poor. Only about 40 percent of Americans have a budget or keep track of their spending. Basic life skills, like budgeting, saving, and investing aren't taught in schools. And while wealth is an enormous privilege that creates incredible opportunities for families, it also comes with a lot of complications. Young people growing up with wealth not only need to learn basic financial literacy. As they get older, they also need to learn about different types of investments, working with professionals, and more.

There's a reason the saying "from shirtsleeves to shirtsleeves in three generations" is repeated so often. It really takes a lot of education and dedicated work to ensure that the second and third generations raised in wealth will steward and grow their family's resources. As an advisor, I have a valuable perspective on this work that I can share with my clients. I've seen other families deal with the same challenges, and I can share best practices.

I talk with my clients a lot about the importance of beginning financial education early and developing both practical skills and a values-based approach to wealth management. I also share resources like a simple family education handbook developed by the private wealth management team at Merrill Lynch.

For clients with young children, I typically recommend starting early with basic financial education, including introducing the idea of charitable giving. That might mean encouraging or requiring kids to donate part of their allowance, taking part in volunteer activities as a family, or talking with kids about the causes the family supports and why.

As children get older, they can begin to take on a formal role in managing the family's wealth. As an advisor, I can help facilitate this education in a few different ways. For example, I might be involved in setting up a trust for the next generation and helping the parents define the terms of that trust. At that planning stage, I can encourage them to think about what they want their children to learn about managing money and the purpose of their wealth as they set up the structures that will provide for the next generation. I can also be directly involved in providing financial education to my clients' children, perhaps by working directly with them to manage a small account or simply sitting down with them for an information session. And as I've mentioned before, I frequently will do things like advise a client's child on the importance of a prenuptial agreement or talk to them about their careers. This kind of high-touch service provides enormous value to clients and helps build client loyalty, as well as helping me build connections with the next generation of the family I'm working with.

The other thing my team and I do that I believe sets us apart is proactively engage all clients in conversations about the purpose of their wealth. Philanthropy is personally very important to me, and I find that almost everyone I meet with is excited to talk about their purpose and values. The purpose of wealth can, of course, include providing for future generations, but I find that most wealthy people also want to have a broader legacy and an impact on causes that they care about. Being an advisor who has experience serving on nonprofit boards and giving to philanthropic causes myself is a real differentiator for me. It helps me attract clients I'm excited to work with.

Developing Rules for Financial Engagement

Wealthy families need to tackle a lot of complicated issues in order to develop a healthy process for managing their money. Who gets a voice in financial decisions? Who gets a vote? How do you balance honoring the legacy of the family's original wealth creator with allowing younger generations to make a mark?

One of the baseline assumptions that goes into family dynamics work is that any decision about money management can either bring family members closer or drive a wedge between them. As you can imagine, this kind of work can quickly get into family therapy territory. Old issues quickly come to light when money is involved.

As advisors, we can work with families in several ways on these issues. My team and I have seen a lot, working with as many wealthy families as we have. We advise clients directly on best practices for making decisions collaboratively as a family. We can talk through thorny questions, like: Does fairness always mean giving every heir the same bequest, or can you be "fair" while tailoring bequests to different people's abilities and needs?

We've also built relationships with some therapists who specialize in family dynamics work, and we regularly refer clients to these professionals. Much like having an estate planning attorney on staff, there's no immediate benefit to my bottom line here. But the long-term payoff of building client loyalty by providing the services my clients urgently need to deal with their top-of-mind issues is invaluable.

Developing a Collaborative Advisory Relationship

My goal is always to build a collaborative relationship with my clients. I'm there to help them achieve their goals, not to tell them what they should do with their money. And in the best-case scenario, I aim to extend this collaborative relationship to include my clients' children as well.

Obviously, you have to approach this topic with great sensitivity and follow your client's lead. But an ideal pattern of engagement might be to start discussions with your client about best practices for financial education when their children are quite young. You can be a source of expert advice on common parenting questions, like allowances, teaching budgeting, and so on. Then, as the children become old enough to start managing some of their own money, you could offer some introductory sessions on budgeting, saving, and investing to teenage or college-age kids, for example.

If you're working with a client with adult children, it's a great idea to ask if they want their adult children to sit in on the occasional meeting. Again, you'll be guided by your primary client's needs and comfort level. But parents of adult children have likely made some kind of estate plan, and it could be useful for the entire family to get an introduction to the current portfolio and the primary client's plans for the future. These kinds of meetings can also be an opportunity to introduce sensitive topics, such as aging and power of attorney. In that case, you're also introducing yourself and beginning to build a relationship with the person who will take over responsibility for financial decisions when your primary client can no longer make those decisions for him- or herself.

In my experience, clients are grateful for the help in educating the next generation on financial matters and on broaching some of these sensitive topics. The next generation also appreciates the clarity around the family's financial position. These are tough topics for families to talk about explicitly. As an advisor, you can help take some of the emotion out of the conversation and steer the family toward an open discussion of practical matters.

A Live Issue for Clients

The bottom line is that this is an issue that many of my clients bring up. It's a high-priority topic for wealthy families, especially for people like most of my clients, who didn't grow up wealthy themselves but are passing on significant wealth to their children.

I had a client bring this up spontaneously in a recent conversation. We hadn't talked about family dynamics before, but in a wide-ranging conversation during a check-in meeting, when I asked him what keeps him up at night, his immediate answer was: "I'm worried about turning my kids into entitled brats."

This guy is type A-plus. He's an incredibly hard worker. We manage about $100 million for him, none of which he inherited from his parents. And he has seven children, ages three to twenty-four, so when he brought this up, I knew this wouldn't be a simple issue for him, given that his kids are at such different stages of their lives.

So, of course, since I'm all about open-ended questions, I simply said, "Tell me more." He started talking about a recent family vacation to Hawaii. They'd flown coach, but the previous year they'd flown first class on a similar trip. One of his daughters complained about flying coach. He was understandably concerned that she was feeling entitled to something that ought to be considered a real privilege.

I told him this is a real issue that many families like his grapple with. I reminded him that if you don't pass on values along with your wealth that wealth will dissipate, just like the old shirtsleeves-to-shirtsleeves saying implies. And I offered to set up a call for him and his oldest children with our family dynamic specialist.

I believe this conversation likely cemented my relationship with this client for the rest of his lifetime. These are the moments that prove that psychology majors make the best financial advisors. In that conversation, it was my ability to listen with an open mind and follow up on an issue that clearly had emotional weight for my client that enabled me to go the extra mile and provide great, differentiating service.

I often say I'm in the peace-of-mind business. And for many of my clients, gaining peace of mind is about making sure their legacies are secure. To help them do that, I have to be willing to dive into these sticky interpersonal issues. Ultimately, family dynamics work helps me build better relationships with my clients, but it also helps me do my job better and deliver what my clients really need: the confidence that their life's work has created lasting value.

Key Takeaways

- My father died two months after I arrived in the United States; he was only fifty-nine when he died.
- Coupled with the shock of the loss was a financial setback for the family, as my father had been the sole breadwinner.
- It's a common story—and one complicated by the difficulty of discussing money among family members.
- As the role of financial planner has evolved over the years, it has become more complicated—and now needs to include family dynamic management.
- For wealthy families, how to educate their children and transfer money to them are tricky issues.
- Wealth managers should be prepared to help.

16

WHY ADVISORS FAIL

It is hard to fail, but it is worse never to have tried to succeed.
—Theodore Roosevelt

Most financial advisors fail in their first few years in business. Imagine if that were true for lawyers or doctors—there'd be a national outcry! Law schools and medical schools would be overhauled, and people by the millions would reconsider what had been thought to be very safe, stable careers.

I believe there's enormous opportunity out there for young people to build successful careers as financial planners. But you can't be complacent. This is a career for self-starters, people with an entrepreneurial mindset, people who get excited when they hear there's no floor to support you as you start out, but there's also no ceiling to limit your rise. If that sounds like you, I truly believe you can build a lucrative career you will love.

So why is the mortality rate so high in this profession? Let's look at a few common reasons financial advisors fail and discuss how you can avoid their mistakes.

They aren't rainmakers.

This is the first and perhaps the biggest reason people fail as financial advisors. A big part of an advisor's job, especially when you're first starting out, is finding and signing new clients. In fact, even as my team has grown, this is still a huge part of my job, after three decades in the business.

A firm like Merrill Lynch can provide you with a lot of resources and support, but they won't just hand you clients on a gilt platter. It's up to you to build your stable of clients. Ultimately, success or failure at attracting clients has nothing to do with where you went to school, how smart you are, or even how successful you are at investing. It's all about your ability to put yourself out there, to take risks, make presentations, and pursue prospects.

A lot of people today seem to believe "selling" is a bad thing. But selling is what makes capitalism work. Selling might have a negative connotation these days, but we're all in the business of selling in one way or another, whether we're literally selling a product, we're selling ourselves to an employer, or we're selling our services to clients.

To me, hard selling is all about the product. The stereotypical pushy car salesperson is irritating because they don't listen to what you, the client, need. They just talk and talk about the product and about all the discounts they can offer. That kind of "selling" *is* a bad thing. But when you focus on the needs of the client, you're not so much selling as you are sharing your insights.

Great financial advisors must be rainmakers, but they don't have to be aggressive salespeople. In fact, the most successful advisors today think of themselves as needs-based consultants. Instead of focusing on selling a product, they're listening to prospective clients, understanding their needs, and sharing information about how they can meet those needs. The process is much more collaborative and much more thoughtful than the cold-calling advisors might have attempted thirty years ago.

Don't think of prospecting as selling. Think of it as *persuasion*. The better you are at communicating and persuading, the more successful you'll be. Persuasion is a necessary skill, and it's particularly crucial for a financial advisor, who must sign clients to build a business.

Anyone can learn the art of persuasion. Practice truly makes perfect—with practice, you can become a better communicator. You can hone your message so it really sticks. You can practice listening and asking better questions, making presentations, and you can even become more charismatic if you concentrate on being present in the conversation. Even now, after three decades in the business, I still practice my pitch in front of a mirror to make sure I convey the right tone and body language. Just try it. It sounds hokey, but you will be amazed how you can improve your presentation.

Practice can make a real difference in your ability to pitch and win clients. But if you can't see yourself spending a good portion of your time identifying prospects and pitching yourself to them, you won't succeed as a financial advisor. You might be better suited to a more behind-the-scenes role, as an analyst, planner, or client services manager.

They hate rejection. When you're first starting out, it's a numbers game. If you're presenting in front of ten people, you might get two of them to sign on as clients. You simply can't expect to sign every prospect as a client—that's just not realistic.

Think about buying a house. No matter how good your real estate agent is, you can only buy one house, and you're almost certainly going to look at a bunch of places that aren't right for you before you find the one that is. Someone who's looking for a new financial advisor won't shop around as much as a prospective home buyer would, but the principle still applies—not every advisor will be right for that client. That's not an objective judgment on the advisor's quality; it's a subjective choice on the client's part.

You must accept that rejection is perfectly normal. This is the mental side of succeeding in this business. Don't take rejection personally. Don't let it send you into a spiral or question whether you're cut out for the business. Instead, take it as a prompt to find ways to improve your pitching strategy. Maybe there's something about your message that didn't resonate, and you can look for ways to refine.

Of course, sometimes it's not you at all. Some people simply aren't ready to work with a financial advisor. Others may have an advisor they're a little dissatisfied with, but they haven't quite gotten to the point where they're ready to make a switch. Sometimes the success or failure of a pitch meeting is all about timing.

Don't overreact to one pitch meeting. But do look for patterns in how your meetings with prospective clients are going. When you identify a pattern, like a particular section of your pitch that doesn't seem to be connecting, you can work to improve. But remember—it is a numbers game. You must get out in front of a lot of prospects in order to successfully build a business.

They're not patient enough. I've seen younger advisors get impatient with the time it takes to build a solid book of business. But that's just the reality—it takes time!

Think about it this way: if your goal is to build a career for thirty or forty years, is it worth it to spend five or ten years working really hard to build that long lasting business? Obviously, I believe it is. For me, the effort I put into building my career has certainly paid off.

And that building phase isn't your whole career. While you'll never stop pitching to new prospects, eventually you will find it gets easier to find those new prospects. Right now, about two-thirds of my new clients come from referrals. I've been at this long enough, and I've been successful enough on my clients' behalf, that my clients are my advocates. They do a lot of my marketing for me these days.

I still prospect every single day. About a third of my new clients still come from working with my team to get our name and our thought leadership out there and make new connections. But I'm not in fast-growth mode anymore, I'm growing more strategically, and I have that built-in marketing engine that comes from having a stable of satisfied clients.

The building phase is hard. It takes time. But if you put in the work, and you're successful in this business, you could be in the top 1 percent of earners in the world. Just don't underestimate the effort required to get to that point. After all, if it were easy, everyone would be doing it.

They hold self-limiting beliefs. If you believe you won't succeed because you don't know any rich people, or because of who you are, those are self-limiting beliefs. If you aren't able to change those beliefs, they will hold you back. You need to come up with a new way of looking at yourself and your prospects.

As discussed earlier in the book, it's true that the financial advisory industry is far too pale and male. But there are two ways of looking at this fact: you could assume that only white men will succeed in the future, or you could see this disparity as an opportunity. After all, the demographics of this country are changing rapidly. There are plenty of young, diverse people out there who are looking for advisors who will understand them and the challenges they face.

Signing new clients is all about persuasion, and persuasion requires confidence. You need to be able to walk into a meeting with a prospective client and convince them that you are a competent professional, you're smart and trustworthy, and you can deliver value like nobody else. How can you project that to a prospect if you don't believe it yourself?

Before I went to prospective client meetings, I used to listen to motivational cassette tapes—yes, cassette tapes. I'd listen to tapes on how to present yourself in a meeting and pick up tips on projecting confidence through body language, so that I'd be as prepared as possible to do a great job. Today I am a voracious consumer of audiobooks and podcasts. It is amazing how much good content is available on virtually any subject. Success isn't all about the practical side of building a list of prospects and delivering value to clients; it's also a mental game.

I had an advisor early in his career come to me for advice about fifteen years ago. He'd grown up in Mexico and had a thick accent. He was afraid prospective clients would be turned off by his accent, and he'd struggle to build a business. I certainly understood his fear. But I encouraged him to turn that belief around and put all his energy into believing that people would love his accent. I also encouraged him to target Latinx clients. I wanted him to turn his perceived weakness into a strength both mentally and practically.

Today he's a very successful advisor. About 50 percent of his clients are Latinx business owners. And he has great success reaching new clients. One of his most successful strategies is attending trade shows—he'll get a booth and share information with the business owners who attend.

What can you do to turn your self-limiting beliefs around? Think about how to attack those negative beliefs both practically and emotionally. If you're concerned you don't look like the stereotypical wealth advisor—in other words, you're not an old white man—you need to work both on reframing that belief for yourself mentally, and on developing practical strategies for turning it into a strength. Create a mantra for yourself that emphasizes how you're bringing a fresh perspective to the industry, and work on targeting clients who will value that fresh perspective. If you work on both your mental and practical game simultaneously, you'll create a virtuous circle, where your increased confidence will help you find success, and each new client you sign will increase your confidence.

They haven't chosen a target market. You can't say that the entire world is your target market. It simply won't work. If you don't target a relatively narrow segment of the market, you won't know where to start to find prospective clients. You'll also be more likely to come across as desperate to prospects, who will pick up on the fact that you'll take anyone and everyone. Like my friend who targeted Latinx clients, you need a market segment to focus on. You can target two or three segments if you like, but you need to narrow your prospects down from everyone.

Say you decide to target medical professionals. Once you've made that decision, you can start to study the characteristics of your target clients. I started out my career targeting doctors, so I know a few things about them, such as their concern about getting sued makes malpractice insurance a priority; that they face death every day means they're more interested in life insurance than others might be; and that they know they live by their skills means they also know disability insurance is important. Of course, every client is different, but having experience with doctors gives me a head start in a conversation with a new prospect.

The more clients you work with in your target market, the

more of an expert you'll become. You'll get to know their needs and interests, and you'll learn where to find them. You'll be able to tailor your presentations more and more to appeal to new prospects in that segment. For example, I know an advisor in New York City who's built a thriving business targeting women who've been divorced. She works with several divorce attorneys. She understands where these women are coming from—in many cases, their husbands handled money matters while they were married, so they have some catching up to do when it comes to financial education. She's become the go-to person for divorced women of that generation in the city. She holds regular seminars on investing that help her meet new prospects.

There are so many different target segments you could pursue: retirees, corporate executives, young professionals, small business owners, real estate investors and more. You might think that limiting yourself to one or two specific demographics would make it harder to find clients. But in fact, when you focus on a narrow market segment, it actually becomes easier to find prospects. And the more expertise you develop in the needs of your target clients, the more you'll develop a reputation as the go-to financial planner for that segment—and the more referrals you'll get.

They're pessimists. If you don't come across as optimistic, you'll struggle to succeed as a financial advisor. Regardless of what's happening in the markets, you're in the business of hopes and dreams. Clients come to you because they have goals. They want to achieve financial independence, or they want to feel confident that they'll be able to take care of their needs in retirement. If you don't project that confidence, how can you expect your clients to be confident about your ability to deliver for them?

Imagine you went to a doctor, and she started talking about

how many people die in their sixties. You'd probably run and never go back, right? It's important to make sure clients understand the risks of any investment, but if you focus only on the downside risks, you'll turn clients away. People come to an advisor because they want to get their financial lives on track. They're looking to you to improve their lives. They want an advisor they can trust who will also help them get to their personal promised land.

People often discount the importance of optimism. In fact, many people seem to think they'll appear more intelligent if they project pessimism. If I wrote a book about why I believe the next twenty years will be the best ever for humanity, would I get on the news?

Pessimism comes from fear. Every investor needs a healthy respect for risk, but if you invest out of fear, you'll end up making bad decisions. In the past thirty years, gold has returned about 1.1 percent, and yet some people cling to it. Why? Because of their pessimism. Because of their fear.

There's something very powerful in the spirit of optimism. Optimism makes you a problem-solver. Optimism gives you a can-do attitude. But if you believe something won't work out, you'll build barriers and allow self-limiting beliefs to hold you back. Success requires hard work, of course, but it also requires a belief that good things are possible.

Key Takeaways

- Most advisors fail in the early years of their business.
- Why?
    - Because they fail at rainmaking.
    - Because they lack patience.
    - Because they have self-limiting beliefs.
    - Because they haven't chosen a target market.
    - Because they are too pessimistic.

17

JUMP-STARTING A STRUGGLING BUSINESS

Have the courage to follow your heart and intuition.
—Steve Jobs

I targeted doctors when I first started out in the wealth management business, but not for a very good reason. I targeted doctors because, at every cocktail party I went to, the people with the best cars were doctors.

I did see an initial burst of success. I think my people skills got me started on the path to growth, and I did at least have a target market in mind, even if I hadn't chosen that segment very scientifically. I could do things like hold seminars at hospitals. I knew where to find my ideal clients.

But after a couple of years, I hit a plateau in my growth. I felt like my career had stalled, and I wasn't growing fast enough. I decided it was time to rebrand and identify a new target market.

This time I did a little more homework than just looking up

and down the street as I walked into a party. I knew that recent regulation changes had begun to make it more common for corporations, particularly tech companies, to compensate employees with stock options. I saw opportunity there for a lot of wealth creation among hardworking people I could relate to, people who hadn't grown up with wealth. So I got a book on stock options—*Consider Your Options: Get the Most from Your Equity Compensation*, by Kaye A. Thomas. I've now read all five editions of this book, and I highly recommend it—and started doing the research that would enable me to become an expert on equity compensation and target this growing new market.

If I had to credit one decision with my future success, it would be that one. Targeting corporate executives with stock options jump-started my business at a time when my growth had slowed. It set me on the path to greater future growth.

My second major pivot point was deciding to impose a minimum account size. When I was starting out, I would work with anyone, but I realized after a while that I didn't like the lifestyle. I felt I couldn't provide the level of service I wanted to when I had five hundred or more clients. I'd have twenty-five or more messages to return every day. I'd end the day behind and end up making calls from home in the evening. Of course, back in those days, I didn't have access to account statements at home. Imposing minimums allowed me to provide better service and develop deeper relationships with a smaller number of clients, and that's been part of what sets my practice apart ever since.

I speak to many advisors who have been in business for a while and have achieved a certain level of success but are now feeling stuck. Their growth has stalled, and they're not sure how to break out into the next level. It's a common problem, and one I can obviously relate to. When you're just starting out, you're fully in growth mode. But if you allow yourself to take your foot off the gas, your business may start to stall out. Or you may simply hit a ceiling and find you need to redefine your target market or change something about how you do business to continue to grow.

Let's walk through some strategies for jump-starting a struggling business:

Redefine your personal purpose and mission. Start by setting aside some time for personal reflection. Ask yourself questions like:

- Why did I get into this business?
- What am I really good at?
- What sets me apart from other advisors?
- Who is my ideal client?
- What would it look like if I achieved fantastic success for that ideal client?

Your purpose should be your true north. Everything you do should be bringing you closer to achieving your purpose. By starting with personal reflection, you can ensure that as you work on improving your business, you're building a business that you can be proud of.

Reassess your value proposition. How would your clients describe what you do? How do they perceive your value-add? Talk to a few clients to get their insights. Most clients will be more than willing to help.

It's easy for you to sit in your office and come up with mission statements and brand statements and tell yourself what sets your practice apart. But ultimately, it's your clients' perception of what you do that defines your brand.

Make this an intentional exercise and start compiling feedback. Look for patterns. If you don't hear the same things from most or all your clients, then you're not establishing a clear brand. If what you're hearing from clients doesn't align with the brand you hope to establish, then you need to do some reflection. Are you falling short of delivering the service you aspire to provide your clients? Or are they recognizing a strength you didn't realize was a differentiator for you?

The harsh truth is that simply being competent isn't a strong enough brand. Doing your job well is the minimum. If all your clients can say about you is that you're dependable and you've managed their investments well, you're in trouble. You need to have a clear differentiator to ensure long-term success in a competitive field.

It may be worth working with a business coach who can help you gather and evaluate feedback and determine next steps. This kind of investment in your business typically pays great dividends.

Assess your strengths and weaknesses. Begin by making a list for yourself. Try to be ruthlessly honest on both sides—really think about what you're good at and where you tend to fall short.

Then get feedback on your list from some people you trust. Think about people who know you personally as well as professional contacts. A team member or colleague could be a great resource, as could a former professor or boss. See how your list resonates with others in your life. Is it accurate? Are you missing anything?

In some cases, a strategic hire can help you overcome a weakness. Maybe you need to hire a client relationship manager to help you stay on top of client communication. Maybe an office manager could help you stay more organized. Or maybe you could call on specialized analysts more often to help you get more visibility into certain asset classes you don't have much experience working with.

Set clear goals. As I've explained, I'm a big fan of goal setting. It's hard to get anywhere if you don't know where you're going. If you find that your growth has stalled, it's time to get serious, and specific, about your goals. Define your growth goals in terms of new households and new assets. Get as detailed as possible: How many sub-$1 million accounts do you want to sign? How many $1 to $5 million? And so on. Be ambitious. If you've never signed a $10 million account before, now is the time to be bold.

Once you have your goals in writing, you can work out your step-by-step plan for achieving them. How will you build your personal brand? Who will you ask for referrals? What specific things can you do to build and work your network? Which local CPAs and attorneys can you trade referrals with? Where can you give presentations and share your expertise?

Identify your marketing strategy. Your marketing strategy needs to be specific to your local community and your target market. What drives wealth creation in your area? What news sources do your ideal clients trust? Where do they congregate? Who are the local influencers they look to? Every market in the country is different, and there is no one-size-fits all approach.

If you're struggling to come up with an effective marketing strategy, go back to the chapter on prospecting and brainstorm some new ways you could reach potential clients. Remember that your current satisfied clients can be great sources of referrals, but only if you ask them to send people your way. The old adage, "You reap what you sow," definitely holds true for this business. You must put in the work to market yourself, ask for referrals, and work your network before you can expect to reap the rewards in new clients.

Call for backup. If your practice is part of a larger firm, talk to your local management team about relaunching your business and revamping your marketing strategy. In my experience, these managers are eager to help you build your practice. They've been trained in business development—they're a great resource.

Don't let pride keep you from asking for support when you need it. Having an experienced team behind you is one of the benefits of working within a larger firm—take advantage of that!

Assess your team. Do you have the team and resources you need to effectively serve your target segments? I strongly believe teams have won out in a big way versus the solo advisor. This business is too complex to be handled by just one or two individuals. If you're finding that you're struggling to keep up with the clients you have, or that your clients often need deeper expertise in certain areas, it may be time to add more people to your team in order to grow.

Of course, it's not easy to create a "dream team" overnight. My advice, if you're not in a position to hire yet, is to create a virtual team that reflects the many dimensions of service you provide to clients. A virtual team might include a senior advisor who helps you land bigger accounts, a lending specialist who can help clients manage debt, an estate planning attorney, a wealth strategist, an investment strategist, some analysts who cover segments your clients gravitate toward, and so on. These can be colleagues at your larger firm or independent professionals you can refer clients to in a mutually beneficial relationship.

Invest in your practice. Investing in your business today will pay off in a big way down the line. For decades, I have reinvested almost 20 percent of my income back into my practice to build the team I need for the future. Over the course of three decades, my practice has grown over 50 percent by following this reinvestment rule. Very few businesses can provide this type of return on your investment. This is the only business in the world in which you can start out without a cent of capital—all you need is your sweat equity, hard work, and determination to succeed.

Even if your practice is part of a larger firm, you should never wait for the firm to give you resources. Investing in yourself shows management you're serious about creating long-term success. A manager told me once that he was willing to invest in my business *because* he saw I was investing. I had skin in the game, and that gave him the confidence to give me more resources. Take yourself seriously, and the people around you will take you seriously too.

Regularly assessing your team will help you determine where to invest these resources. Something as simple as hiring an assistant to help manage your schedule, or a business manager who can provide you leverage by assuming the responsibility of administration and client service, could help you grow your business to the next level.

Learn to delegate. This is a big one. A lot of advisors stop growing because they don't know how to hire, and when they do hire, they don't know how to trust the people they've hired. You only have so many hours in your day. If you can't turn tasks over to your team, you can't grow. You must be able to delegate, and that means you have to allow people to make mistakes as they learn. As a leader, your job should be to articulate goals and then step aside to allow your team to work. They can come to you with problems, but you should not be micromanaging their day-to-day work. That defeats the purpose of building a team.

Delegation is not abdication. You need to set up regular meetings to review client objectives and outstanding tasks and assess opportunities. You're still the team leader. You just need to let people do the work you've hired them to do.

The goal is to build a team that's greater than the sum of its parts—a team in which everyone's strengths complement one another and create something truly great. Personally, I know I'm great at drawing up business plans and developing a vision for my team. But I also know my weakness is in the granular details of administration. Remember how miserable I was when I had five hundred clients and was spending my life returning messages? I do. I solved this problem by hiring a supercompetent business manager who supervises our entire client service team and is charged with process and execution. Now I can do what I do best, and I can trust my team to be strong where I'm weak. Trust the people you hire for your team, delegate with confidence, and give them the ability to grow and make mistakes.

Trust your team. Treat every single member as a partner. In my practice, after a gestation period of two years, every member is part of our profit-sharing plan.

Think of yourself as the CEO of a start-up company. You can only attract the best people by making them a part owner of the practice. My average team member has been with me for over fifteen years, and I strongly believe that longevity is due to three principles our team fervently believes in: shared values, shared responsibilities, and shared rewards.

Think carefully before merging with another practice. If you are a solo practitioner, you may be tempted to merge with another advisor to form a team. Partnerships can be a great move in some cases, but I'd advise against shotgun marriages. Teaming and partnership require careful assessment, and it may make sense to hire a professional coach or consultant to come up with the right criteria you should be looking for in a partner. Compatibility and trust are often more important than simple competence in a team arrangement. If that sounds like a marriage, there's a reason for that. A business partnership requires a lot of trust and mutual respect, and you can't rush those things.

On the other hand, I am a big advocate of strategic partnerships to win a piece of business. Remember: you can construct a virtual team with a senior advisor or specialist to pursue new business opportunities. Sometimes a strategic partnership may end up in a more permanent arrangement because you have had an opportunity to work with another advisor and see them in action—you've had the opportunity to build that trust and mutual respect.

Commit to growth. Some advisors stop growing because they've gotten to a point where they're comfortable with their income. It's wonderful to have reached a point in your career where you feel confident that you can support your family and your lifestyle, but I honestly believe it's a mistake to let yourself coast. I think a commitment to growth energizes your practice, motivates your team, and keeps you sharp in a highly competitive world.

Committing to growth doesn't mean you have to put in twenty extra hours a week. With a great team behind you, you can maintain the lifestyle you enjoy and keep pushing to grow your business. Bringing more younger advisors onto your team and gradually giving them more and more responsibility can be a great way to infuse your practice with fresh energy without you having to push yourself beyond your limits.

Key Takeaways

- If you are struggling to grow, analyze demographic trends and follow the money.
- When you can afford to, set a minimum account size.
- Redefine your purpose and mission; reassess your value proposition.
- Assess your strengths and weaknesses.
- Set clear goals and strategies.
- Assess your team; invest in your practice.
- Learn to delegate and trust your team.
- Commit to growth.

18

ALIGNING MIND, BODY, AND SPIRIT FOR LONG-TERM SUCCESS

The great philosopher and spiritual teacher B. K. S. Iyengar once said, "Health is a state of complete harmony of the body, mind, and spirit." Health is important to anyone, of course, but I believe this kind of complete health of mind, body, and spirit is particularly important for financial advisors.

As an advisor, you are expected to be in a high-performance mode all the time. Clients expect you to be up-to-date on economic events, and to have a smart take on what they mean for investment strategy and long-term financial planning. They also look to you to maintain a sense of optimism in the face of crisis and uncertainty.

Advisors are also entrepreneurs. As an advisor, you work for yourself—your business grows and thrives when you're on top of our game. Even when you have a team behind you, you're the leader, and you're largely responsible for setting direction and motivating the team. If you get overwhelmed or burned out, your business will suffer.

People gravitate to advisors for insight and wisdom in a world overwhelmed with data and information. Stress is part of our daily lives. If you don't manage your stress well, it can wear you down and lead to serious medical issues.

So how can an advisor be at the top of their game all the time? This is where the mind, body, and spirit become supremely important. We are at our best when our personal lives are in balance and our minds, bodies, and spirits are fully aligned.

This is a subject I'm passionate about. Let's walk through some ideas on how to align each of these areas to promote long-term success.

Mind

For over forty years, I have been a meditator. Specifically, I practice Transcendental Meditation, also called TM. There are many ways to meditate, but TM is the technique that resonated with me because of how simple and effortless I have found it to be. Bob Roth, one of the best teachers in the world, describes TM in his book *Strength in Stillness*: "The Transcendental Meditation technique has many purposes: reduce stress, clear the mind, raise performance."

It is not easy to get into the habit of daily meditation. For the first several years, my practice was erratic. But once I found my groove, I began to meditate every single day. Now, every morning,

I spend twenty to thirty minutes in quiet meditation. It helps me clear the cobwebs from my mind and provides me clarity of thought and purpose. For me, it's like wiping the slate clean every day, erasing my fears and concerns and allowing me to start a new day infused with a sense of wonder, optimism, and positive expectation.

My goal this year is to start meditating a second time after work to clear my head after the day and put myself into a calm and present frame of mind, so I can have a better evening with my family. I find meditation gives new energy to my evening after a day's work.

Over time, the practice of meditation has become an essential part of my being and is woven into my daily routine. I often tell my children that the gift of mediation is a greater legacy than material wealth. We are actually a family of meditators. All six of us in our family have embraced meditation, though we all practice different techniques—TM, mindfulness, Buddhist meditation, mediation using an app, and more. It does not matter what technique you embrace. Over time, you will gravitate to the method that most resonates with you.

Meditation has helped me enormously in every dimension of my life. I think it has made me more self-aware and reflective in my interactions with family, friends, my team, and the world at large. Of course, I'm not perfect. That's not the goal. All I am suggesting is that meditation has grounded me and has helped me create a mental framework to deal with the stresses and challenges of life. Meditation helps me renew my defining purpose every single day.

Even if you don't practice meditation, remaining centered and self-aware is crucial to success in this business. I believe most people place too much emphasis on IQ and not enough on EQ, or emotional intelligence. If you focus too much on IQ, you end up with young people entering the workforce who are great with spreadsheets but terrible at relating to their coworkers.

Some of the most successful people I've met in my life have only average IQs, but their emotional intelligence is off the charts. Over time, I have found that EQ is far more important, because success is all about working with people. Financial advisors need empathy, understanding, active listening, and communication.

Ultimately, EQ is the ability to deal with people and circumstances. As an advisor, you are always confronted with issues of one kind or another—a market correction, an administrative issue, a client who is unhappy with a tax statement, a delay on K-1s, and so on. My advice to my team is to always confront an issue, not run away from it. Most things can be fixed—with a little emotional intelligence. First, listen with intent to your client and understand the situation. Do not express anger or resentment or be defensive in any way. All feedback from a client is valid, whether you think it has any merit or not. Listen first, express empathy, and set expectations on when they can expect to hear from you with a solution.

I also encourage my team members to share concerns with each other. It takes some EQ to admit that you're struggling, but in my experience, you almost always get a helpful answer when you bring a problem to a colleague. No team member is an island unto themselves. Encouraging constant communication and sharing of best practices must be part of your team's culture.

As a leader, I've always believed that emotional intelligence is one of my greatest assets. Not to brag, but I recently had a team member who was leaving tell me that she didn't know if she'd ever work with another boss as good as me. I've always believed that getting the best out of people is all about respect. People know I'm the boss—I don't need to create a command-and-control culture to get results.

I had an advisor who worked with me who was supersmart, but everyone complained about him when he joined the team. When he needed help from the team with a client situation, he'd just tell people what to do. He wouldn't share any background about who the client was or what their goals were. He believed he was being efficient—but how efficient is it to alienate your team? We worked together on emotional intelligence and people skills, and he saw much more success when he started treating everyone as an equal partner.

Focusing on emotional intelligence, self-reflection, and mindfulness doesn't mean practicing self-denial. I am a big believer in the pursuit of happiness. But to me, happiness is the result of living by your convictions and engaging in a purposeful endeavor. I find great satisfaction in helping a client understand a strategy, helping them achieve their cherished goals, and generally being a problem-solver and guide for them. For me, happiness is a result of helping others find their direction. Happiness is helping a weak team member succeed. Happiness is sharing rewards generously with your team. Happiness is helping every team member succeed and achieve their potential. Self-reflection can help you identify your purpose and help you pursue happiness in the ways that will be most meaningful to you.

Body

It's easy to let things like diet and exercise fall by the wayside when you're busy with a demanding job. But taking care of your body is crucial. I really believe in the old saying "your body is your temple." You must eat right, get regular exercise, and get enough rest in order to be at your best. If your body isn't healthy, you won't be able to do your job well over the long term. Eventually, your poor health will start to undermine you.

Taking care of your body isn't just about diet, exercise, and rest either. In addition to IQ and EQ, "physical intelligence" is emerging as a major determinant of success and happiness. In their new book *Physical Intelligence,* Patricia Peyton and Claire Dale describe PQ as "the active management of our physiology—the ability to detect and strategically influence the balance of chemicals in our bodies and brains."

This means working to understand all the factors that help you maintain physical and mental balance. It means managing stress and anxiety in healthy, effective ways. It means preserving time for your relationships, hobbies, and the things that make your life rich and meaningful. Ultimately, it means practicing active self-care.

Self-care has become a buzzword in recent years, and as a result I think it's often misunderstood. Taking care of yourself does not just mean pampering or indulging yourself, and it definitely doesn't just mean buying yourself a treat. Truly taking care of yourself is about having the self-awareness to know what keeps you in balance. Depending on your circumstances, taking care of yourself might mean blocking out time for exercise even in a busy week, avoiding screens for thirty minutes before bed to ensure restful sleep, or starting every day with a walk outside.

Work on building your own physical intelligence so that you know what triggers that sense of imbalance in your mind and body, and how to bring yourself back into balance. There are some simple exercises that work for everyone, like improving your posture, breathing deeply, and taking movement breaks throughout a day spent at a computer. There's also plenty of research out there on scientifically proven ways to reduce your stress, including meditation, spending time in nature, and periodically putting down your devices and spending some disconnected time alone or with friends or family. Your goal should be to find the techniques that work best for you and practice them regularly so that you can always be physically able to do your best.

Spirit

I'm a practical person—most financial advisors are. But I believe, as the Iyengar quote I opened this chapter with suggests, true health is more than physical and mental. True health is a balance of mind, body, and spirit.

I'm not here to tell you how to manage the spiritual dimension of your life. But there is one spiritual practice that is appropriate in any faith tradition, or none, and that I believe is particularly crucial for financial advisors: gratitude.

As an immigrant, I feel enormously fortunate to live in a great country like ours. America is a powerful dream and embodies a strong immigrant ethic. Most of us, or our ancestors, came from different parts of the world to build a new life in this country. Although we have seen polarization in political views in the past decade, there are many wonderful virtues that bind us together, and my hope is that we continually work on forging a just society and creating opportunity for all citizens.

For me, philanthropy is a way of expressing that gratitude. I believe those of us who have been blessed with wealth have an obligation to give back as a way of expressing our gratitude for all the gifts we've been given in this life. My team shares a strong belief in giving back to causes that benefit our local communities and the world at large.

I spend a significant portion of my time working to support causes that are personally meaningful to me. Having grown up in India, I feel a sense of responsibility to do my best to help those in need. For years, I looked for a transparent way to give back to India, but most charities I encountered were personal projects. So, when the American India Foundation was founded, after the Gujarat earthquake in 2001, I was eager to get involved. Merrill Lynch supported the organization's first fundraising gala, and my wife and I were instrumental in founding the Boston chapter after a visit to India in 2004.

The primary mission of AIF is disrupting poverty in India and enhancing the lives of the underprivileged. Over the past two decades, AIF has emerged as one of the leading diaspora-inspired organizations in the United States. In 2020 we led an effort to raise over $2 million to provide much-needed oxygen equipment to alleviate the Covid crisis in India.

In 2004 I visited my hometown of Hyderabad with my wife, Nalini, and my four young children. I was starting to become concerned that my kids were growing up so privileged. It's all too easy to become lulled into thinking that things like Caribbean vacations are normal. So, while we were traveling, we visited a girl's school in a poor neighborhood where the American India Foundation had piloted a program called Digital Equalizer. The goal was to provide computers and internet access to bridge the digital divide.

The students created a special presentation for us on a science project. All of us were blown away by the optimism and resourcefulness of these kids who just happened to be born into poverty. I particularly remember my son saying, "I couldn't do that," even with all the resources he had at the wonderful school he attended. The visit made a deep impression on all of us, including our children. I believe experiences like that helped shape my children's values and encourage them to make giving back a part of their lives.

India will always have a call on my heart, but I also believe strongly in working in the communities in which I live. Many years ago, I was introduced to the Boston Harbor Islands, a wonderful natural resource of thirty-four islands surrounding Boston. My wife encouraged me to join the board of directors, due to her strong interest in environmental preservation. This has been a wonderful experience for me, serving on the board and leading the organization as chair. During my time with the organization, we were able to get the islands declared a national park, meaning they will be preserved as green spaces for all to enjoy forever.

In our local town of Sharon, my kids were involved in their high school years in an organization called Youth Lead, a youth leadership group that encouraged respectful dialogue and discussion on some of the most contentious issues of our time, including income inequality, racism, and religious intolerance. I saw the profound impact Youth Lead had on shaping our children's perspective on the world. They made great friends through the organization and learned that they needed to work to understand people who were different from them better.

My wife joined the board to help the organization succeed. Several years later, when they ran into financial problems, I stepped in as chair to help launch a community fundraising drive to stabilize the finances. Today Youth Lead is a thriving organization under the aegis of Emerson College in Boston. Recently, I had the distinct honor of being nominated to the board of The Boston Foundation (TBF), one of the oldest and most prestigious community foundations in the country. TBF is dedicated to creating a more equitable city and region. I hope to learn more about community partnerships and interact with philanthropists on their mission and purpose.

Philanthropy is truly a family activity for us. My wife and I both work to support the Museum of Fine Arts in Boston. My mother is a longtime supporter of Meals on Wheels, and until she was ninety she was out making deliveries every other day. Giving back has also become important to my kids—they each support causes that they believe in, in their own ways.

I make it a point not to prospect or look for clients in the organizations I am involved in. Over time, however, I have received numerous unsolicited referrals from my philanthropic ecosystem. I guess you can call it good karma.

In my wealth management practice, nothing gives me more joy and satisfaction than introducing our clients to philanthropy. Educating clients on the benefits of philanthropy, from both altruistic and economic angles, is a regular part of my practice. I strongly believe philanthropy strengthens the bonds between family members and provides them an opportunity to collaborate around a common vision.

With the tremendous performance of the equity markets over the last decade, donor advised funds (DAF) and family foundations have proliferated. But our work really begins after a vehicle like that is established. My team is actively engaged with clients on developing a purpose, mission, and strategy for their philanthropic capital. We hold educational webinars for our clients on philanthropy and introduce them to local community foundations.

Recently we had a conversation with a client, a widower worth over $100 million. Over the years, he had generously provided for his children and grandchildren using strategies such as a dynasty trust, a GRAT (grantor-retained annuity trust), and other gifting vehicles. Since he has used his lifetime exemption, he realized his family would be faced with a massive estate tax bill on his passing, potentially over 50 percent.

We introduced him to the concept of a CLAT (charitable lead annuity trust). With this vehicle, he can get an upfront deduction, the charity of his choice will receive annuity payments for a set number of years, and the remaining assets pass on to his children without any gift or estate taxes. He is now in the process of establishing both a living and testamentary charitable lead trust.

Our wealth strategists were closely involved in the entire process, working with external attorneys to draft legal documents. In effect, we showed this client a great way to benefit charity and family at the same time, almost eliminating all estate taxes and benefitting the world at the same time. This kind of work is incredibly rewarding for me—it's another way that I can give back by encouraging others to do the same.

Key Takeaways

- Health of mind, body, and spirit is very important for financial advisors, who can be on call 24-7.
- I practice meditation and recommend you find a practice along the same lines.
- EQ (emotional quotient) is more important than IQ (intelligence quotient) for success in the financial management business.

- PQ (physical quotient, or "physical intelligence") is also important.

- I believe in practicing gratitude.

- Philanthropy has been an important part of my business philosophy. I never solicit people while working in a philanthropic organization, but I often get unsolicited requests from people I meet during this work.

- Setting up philanthropic organizations for my clients has also been an important and satisfying part of my work.

Conclusion

SOME FINAL THOUGHTS

The wealth management business has changed a lot since I first joined the business, and it will continue to evolve over time. Automation and robo-advisors will increase their market share, but they'll never replace the human touch and emotional connection an advisor can provide. A good advisor is an anchor in times of distress and a trusted confidante. Personalized advice will always have a crucial role to play. The key to survival and success for financial advisors will lie in our ability to anticipate needs and provide meaningful solutions to the problems our clients face.

In my opinion, the defining need for families today is the entire spectrum of family dynamic and legacy planning—developing a mission statement for family wealth, creating a consensus around philanthropy and governance, resolving different points of view within a family regarding the purpose of wealth, respecting and understanding different political and social viewpoints of family members, and creating a legacy of empowerment, not entitlement.

These are difficult issues to address, and advisors need to get proficient in the art of communication, from messaging to active listening. This is not something you want to totally delegate to an outside coach or psychologist. They can be important allies, but as an advisor, you need to own and drive the process. It is important to remember that your client has selected you to lead them to a better place for their families for generations to come. When you advise with purpose, always focusing on positive outcomes for your clients, the planets will align for your personal success and happiness.

Financial advisors are not just investment managers. Our role is multidimensional: family dynamics, tax optimization, estate and legacy strategy, philanthropy, asset and liability management, business services, and risk management. Perhaps the most important service we provide is emotional support. In his new book, *Noise: A Flaw in Human Judgment*, Nobel Prize–winning author Daniel Kahneman shows that decisions by people and organizations are variable and inconsistent, often influenced by the emotions of the moment. As advisors, we need to be the steady hand during a market crisis and display a quiet sense of confidence in the overall strategy. Some of the best advisors I know had backgrounds in psychology and sociology.

The business of wealth management is more professional and transparent today than ever before. But we still have more to accomplish. We need to continually innovate to deliver solutions for our clients' short- and long-term objectives. In addition, we need to be radically transparent and fair in pricing our services. If you relentlessly focus on achieving positive client outcomes and delivering the elusive peace of mind that clients hope for, you will be successful beyond your wildest imagination.

ACKNOWLEDGMENTS

I am profoundly grateful to my company, Merrill Lynch, for giving me the opportunity to build a truly fulfilling life and career. And kudos to the members of the Sharma Group—my second family My team has been an essential part of my journey of the past three decades. There is no way I could have accomplished so much without their arduous work, dedication, and commitment to our shared values and goals.

There are so many folks I need to acknowledge and thank for being partners and advocates in my journey. Most importantly, my amazing wife, Nalini, who has been my source of strength, inspiration, and encouragement from day one at Merrill Lynch. She has always given me unfiltered advice on my business and helped me focus on being authentic and true to my convictions.

Many thanks to my wonderful friend and prolific author, physician, and motivational speaker, Dr. Sanjiv Chopra, for his encouragement and advice at every stage of this book. I would also like to thank Dr. Saj-nicole Joni, Dr. Venkat Srinivasan, Steve Kaufman, and Paul Pagnato for their feedback and suggestions.

To my four wonderful children—Meara, Neil, Jay, and Tara—thanks for keeping me grounded and focused on the big picture. You are constantly educating and challenging me to be a better person, and for that I am most grateful. A special thank-you to Meara and Tara, my talented daughters, for their ideas and suggestions on making this book more relevant to young people.

My gratitude to my mother, Mangalam, who was our family's first financial services professional. She was an insurance agent to schoolteachers when we were growing up. Mom continues to be an incredible role model for our family with her caring demeanor and equanimity. I also want to acknowledge my siblings, in particular my younger brother, Steve, for his authentic feedback and second opinion in my various endeavors, from radio DJ to advisor.

This book would not have seen the light of day without the enormously talented father-daughter team of Nick and Sarah Morgan. Over the past year, we have spent countless hours discussing the content, structure, and theme of this book. I am most appreciative of their patience and valuable insights in shaping this book.

I want to acknowledge Merrill's president and my dear friend, Andy Sieg, for encouraging me every step of the way in this book project, from initial concept to completion. A special word of thanks to Steve Samuels for helping me navigate the various steps needed for approval of this book. My gratitude to my Merrill colleagues, Susan Axelrod, Peter Stack, and Selena Morris Defusco, for their diligence and guidance in the entire process.

A big salute to R. J. Shook for enhancing the advisory profession through his pioneering work in developing advisory rankings and promoting best practices.

There are many others in my Merrill Lynch journey I would like to acknowledge for their contributions to my career. First and foremost is my friend, confidante, and business partner of twenty-five years, Chris Kemp. In no particular order, I want to acknowledge the contributions of the following individuals who have served our team with distinction: Ken Sharma, the late Catherine Todd, Ellen Stebbins, Deanna Riccitelli, Cyndi Mulcahy, Christina Zine, Joy Casserly, Kyle Chase, Paul Garrido, Amit Chandra, Marc Marotta, Kris Kalish, Brian Stanton, Janet Kim, Sue Amalanayagam, Amanda Bellone, Toni Haskins, Corey Livingston, Liz Flynn, Erica Zhen, Charu Narain, Daniel Castillo, Jacob Reilly, Brittany Lecolst, and Amy Hallal. Special thanks to my dear friend Ravi Subramanian, from my radio days in India, for sharing his branding and promotional expertise.

There are several key managers who have aided my success in this firm: the late Bob Spangler, who gave me a break in this business; Paul Fehrenbach Sr., who supported my prospecting efforts in my initial years; Jerry Miller, who connected me to key people in the firm; Merril Pyes, who believed in our team's mission; Paul Bowes, who provided wonderful administrative support; Doug Ederle, who has always been so kind and enthusiastic; and my dynamic manager Greg McGauley, who has been a partner, cheerleader, and collaborator for the past fifteen years.

There are several colleagues who I greatly respect and have had the opportunity to interact with over the years to share ideas and best practices: Don Plaus, Augie Cenname, Dana Locniskar, Bhadresh Shah, Frank Migliazzo, the late Hagood Ellison, John Olson, Jeff Erdmann, Pat Dwyer, Paul Guidoboni, Erica Zhen, Raj Bhatia, Tom Vacheron, John Thiel, Gary McGuirk, Guido Graf, Bill King, Rich Pluta, Mike Mara, Kent Pierce, Richard Jones,

Steve Dicarlo, George Bianco, Peter Danas, and Subha and Jim Barry. If I have inadvertently missed anyone, please forgive me.

SUGGESTED BOOKS FOR FURTHER READING

Enlightenment Now: The Case for Reason, Science, Humanism, and Progress by Steven Pinker

Factfulness: Ten Reasons We're Wrong About the World—and Why Things Are Better Than You Think by Hans Rosling with Ola Rosling and Anna Rosling Rönnlund

Kiss That Frog!: 12 Great Ways to Turn Negatives into Positives in Your Life and Work by Brian Tracy and Christina Tracy Stein

The Courage to Act: A Memoir of a Crisis and Its Aftermath by Ben S. Bernanke

Stocks for the Long Run: The Definitive Guide to Financial Market Returns and Long-Term Investment Strategies by Jeremy J. Siegel

Style Investing: Unique Insight into Equity Management by Richard Bernstein

The Intelligent Investor: The Definitive Book on Value Investing by Benjamin Graham

Strength in Stillness: The Power of Transcendental Meditation by Bob Roth

An Autobiography: The Story of My Experiments with Truth by Mahatma Gandhi

Abundance: The Future Is Better Than You Think by Peter H. Diamandis and Steven Kotler